GW00771439

On the Record

On the Record

From Whistleblower to Champion
of Mental Health Care

Ella Curry, Ph.D. RN

Library of Congress Control Number:		2021914668
ISBN:	Hardcover	978-1-6641-8613-2
	Softcover	978-1-6641-8597-5
	eBook	978-1-6641-8596-8

Print information available on the last page.

Rev. date: 08/09/2021

To order additional copies of this book, contact:
Xlibris
844-714-8691
www.Xlibris.com
Orders@Xlibris.com
815170

This memoir shares the journey of a pioneering mental health professional who became the first African American woman to head a major mental hospital in America.

From hospital volunteer (St. Mary's Hospital in 1953 Athens, Georgia) to executive head of several Midwestern and northeastern health care facilities, Dr. Ella Curry left an indelible mark on the leadership in mental healthcare for over six decades.

***Nurse's Week* 1975**
Ella A. Curry, Ph.D., RN (1975)

Dr. Ella Curry is a registered psychiatric nurse with a Ph.D. in Behavioral Healthcare; a Master's in Health Care Administration Management; a Bachelor's in Nursing Management; and a basic Nursing Diploma from the University Hospital (Augusta, GA) under the auspices of The University of Georgia in her home town, Athens, Georgia.

Dr. Curry held positions of increasing administrative responsibility as Army Nurse and Veterans Administrative Nurse Executive for the U. S. Government.

In 1972 she joined the State of Illinois Department of Mental Health as a South Chicago Sub-Regional Director and eventually rose to the position of Executive Director of the Manteno State Hospital, in 1975.

In 1978 she served as the Executive Director of the South Suburban Tinley Park Mental Health Center in Tinley Park, Illinois.

In 1979, Dr. Curry joined the State of New York Office of Mental Health as the Associate Director of The Bronx Psychiatric Hospital. She also served as a Consultant to the Department of Corrections as Mental Health Program Director.

In the early 1980's, Dr. Curry was appointed Executive Director of the Staten Island Developmental Center, formerly known as Willowbrook State School. The account of Dr. Curry's tenure at Willowbrook is the assignment that she considered highlighting in Episode Four of her memoir, "From Whistleblower to Safety." Due to her investigation of corruption and crime at the facility, Dr. Curry felt as if she was "Running from the Mob." Somewhat amazed at her "due diligence" when confronting challenges, her ratifiers often referred to her as the Angela Lansbury of Mental Health.

In recognition of her achievements in meeting the goals of the Willowbrook Consent Decree, Dr. Curry received several citations and awards:

1981 – Acknowledgment by the National Council of Negro Women of Staten Island, for her role in the liberation struggle and efforts toward securing the American Dream.

STATEN ISLAND ADVANCE, Monday, February 16, 1981

Council for Brotherhood

From the left, Dr. Ella Curry, director of the Staten Island Developmental Center; the Rev. Vincent Cuestas, pastor of Bethel Community Church, Tompkinsville.; Yvonne Schmedes, chairman, and Sheila T. Etheridge, president of the Staten Island Section, National Council of Negro Women, help themselves to the buffet at a Brotherhood service in Bethel Community Church.
S.I. Advance Photo by Irving Silverstein

Luncheon: National Council of Negro Women S. I., NY(1981)

1982 – The Harold Piepenbrink Administrator of the Year Award, from the Association of Mental Health Administrators, Cape Code, MA, for outstanding leadership as its president

1983 – Certificate of Appreciation for meeting the goals of the Willowbrook Consent Decree

June 6, 1983 – The Staten Island Borough President Anthony B. Gaeta's Proclamation designating June 6, 1983, Ella A. Curry Day, for compliance with the Willowbrook Consent Decree. Revlon Health Care Group's Declaration of Ella Curry, Woman of the Year, for contributions in the field of mental health.

JANUARY/FEBRUARY 1983

REVLON HEALTH CARE GROUP

Dr. Ella Curry.

A Woman Of The Year

Will Curry, Section Head, Protein Biochemistry, has many good reasons to be proud of his wife, Ella. Last October, there was another.

At that time, Ella, who has a Ph.D. in mental health administration, was honored as Administrator of the Year by a national organization, the Association of Mental Health Administrators.

Since November 1980, Dr. Curry has served as Director of the Staten Island Developmental Center, formerly known as Willowbrook. Previously, she was Associate Director of the Bronx Psychiatric Center and, from 1975 to 1978, was Director of Illinois' largest mental health and mental retardation facility, the Manteno Mental Health Center. That last post made her the first black woman in the nation to be named director of a major mental health institution, according to the Congressional Record.

In addition to the demands of their professional lives, the Curry's have also found the time to raise four children.

DEDICATION

Will Marlvin Curry, Capt.; USAR 1959

This labor of love, duty, and principle is dedicated to my husband, Will (Willie) Marlvin Curry. During our sixty-three (63) years of marriage, Will has been an unwavering source of strength through the most difficult and trying of times. Always he celebrates my courage and tenacity. His words motivate me to follow my dreams. Especially during the past ten years Will has been my principal advocate, encouraging me to inspire others via my career highlights and experiences.

After all this time, I continue to be sustained by this extraordinary man: this husband, father of four, grandfather of seven, and great-grandfather of five. Our love seems stronger than ever. I sincerely thank him for our remarkable years together thus far, and for the wonderful years to come.

ACKNOWLEDGMENTS

Several individuals provided invaluable assistance in helping me recollect then outline my path to the promise that I dreamed of reaching as a young woman. I acknowledge the role of a Higher Being for placing my husband, Will Curry, in my life. Will has stood beside me through jubilation as well as through strife. I am grateful to my sons Tony Curry and the late Joseph E. (Joey) Curry (d. 2014); and to my stepchildren, Hallie and Willie Curry, for their valued and generous advice and research assistance; for their recollections of events and details of our adventures as a family and winning team.

Thanks also go to my extended family, colleagues, and friends for sparking an interest in me to expand my professional reach and realm when all I wanted to do in semi-retirement was to play Bridge, go on cruises with my children and grandchildren, and become a gourmet cook. Finally, I give nods to my granddaughter Kim Lucas and niece Sherry McCurry, Pharm.D.; Jean McCurry; and to my friend, Dr. Velma Price Smith, a retired professor of English, all of whom, upon learning about my odyssey, pushed me to write my story down for the benefit of talented and ambitious young women of color as well as for others in quest of promising career launches and landings.

Finally, a special thanks to my Curry Family:

The Lucien (Hallie) Dorsey Family

The Willie (Lynce) Lucas Family

The Anthony (Carolyn) (and Triplets) Curry Family

The Kevin (Beverly) Lucas Family

The Christopher (Sarah) Dorsey Family

The Doctors (Ugo and Faith) Ihekweazu Family

The Lacy Johnson Family

The Joe Boyd (Malcolm (d. 2021) and Janean) McCurry Family

The Hugh (Dr. Janice) Peyton Family

ABOUT THE AUTHOR

(Introduction)

Literally everything was right in my world in the summer of 1952. I was the pampered fifteen-year-old daughter of doting Black parents and devoted grandparents. Unlike Cinderella, I even had an adoring half-sister, Lacy A. Lattimore, my father's daughter from an earlier relationship. When Lacy was approximately fourteen, her mother, Queen Callaway, moved to Philadelphia, and my mother was more than happy to welcome my sister into the Ben Adams family unit.

Lacy, approximately 11; Ella, 8.

That unforgettable June, I was savoring my customary vacation with my paternal grandparents in Milledgeville, Georgia. My routine there was to share the activities of the couple, who were the pastor and first lady of First A.M. E. Church, in Milledgeville, the location of the infamous Milledgeville Insane Asylum. At the time, Grandpa, The Reverend Eugene Adams, also served as the Acting Bishop of the South East Georgia A.M. E. Church Council.

My grandpa and grandmother, Mrs. Ella Rhea Adams, gave me a very important duty during my visit--that of updating the list of asylum patients whose family members were members of Grandpa's church.

Grandma Ella would prepare baskets and boxes of fried chicken, vegetables, pies, and cakes for the patients in clean white ironed coverings, and I would make lemonade, with lots of sugar, in gallon jugs. A church steward or stewardess transported Grandpa and me to the colored wards of the asylum in a big black car that I named "Betsy". The hospital staff and Betsy's driver would bring in the food, letters and gifts from family and parishioners. For the patients Grandma Ella Adams also saved and sent church bulletins, programs, and some then-dated, Milledgeville daily newspapers.

Inside the facility, we would be escorted to two separate dining halls, one for each gender. The sparsely furnished dining halls were equipped with long tables with white butcher's paper rolled out as table cloths. The windows were secured with bars and half-screen fans, and the wall hangings consisted of insect glue to trap flies. The patients would be dressed in clean gowns of various colors. The men and women in straightjackets would be seated at separate tables from each other and from the general population. A Bible that First A.M.E kept in the women's ward would be brought in for devotion, and Grandpa would pray and read some passages of scripture.

As I surveyed the environment, I thought to myself, Is this what happens when you go to Hell? I wouldn't answer my question, of course. Instead, I would smile and pray and drink my lemonade.

I could hardly wait to return to the parish and tell Grandma Ella about what I witnessed. After Sunday School each Sunday, she would give the Bible study group at First A.M.E a report about our visit.

The third Sunday of my vacation, my mother died, out of the blue—at age 32. Upon hearing the unbearable news, I announced that we would skip going to the Milledgeville Hospital. I had to go home, to Athens, Georgia.

How such a tragedy could happen to such a perfectly contented teenager plunged me into disbelief. This could not be. Yes, my mom had been scheduled for minor surgery, but nothing accounted for this outcome: her having died due to an allergic reaction to anesthesia. I was left with all kinds of questions—medical ones, for the most part. How? Why? What? became the obsessions of the remainder of my teen years. And who could I turn to for answers?

No responses were immediately forthcoming. After my mother's funeral, the adults were in deep discussion as to what should happen to "Little Tootsie," everyone's favorite nickname for me. The grownups discovered that my mother had left a will, bequeathing the house that she had inherited from her adoptive parents to "Little Tootsie." My mother's life insurance and Social Security benefits were left to me as well.

My mother in grass skirt. Hawaii, 1951

With those bombshells, an endless conflict between my father and me developed and spiraled out of control. A battle for my custody ensued between him and my maternal aunt and her husband, who had no children. Eventually the court remanded me to my father's supervision, since he was designated my legal guardian.

In the face of such mounting drama and turmoil, I looked inside myself for the wherewithal to set the world on its axis again.

In eleventh grade, I learned that girls interested in going into the medical field might volunteer at St. Mary's Hospital in my home town (Athens, Georgia) to assist the nurses and medical staff as Candy Stripers. As I trailed the professionals in various departments in the facility, I convinced myself that I was helping to care for someone else's mom when there probably had been no teenager who made my mother feel comfortable during her hospital stay. I wanted to go beyond the call of duty, to do my part in restoring the patients to sound health, especially women and mothers.

There was more: strong mental and emotional stirrings were compelling me to make health care my life's work. With some formal (academic) preparation in the field, perhaps I could delve into some of the areas that the medical professionals overlook or slight when patients blindly put their trust in them. In my mind, these authorities hold life and death in their power. No job was more serious or important than this. What could I contribute?

After graduating from high school in 1953, I enrolled in the nursing program at the University of Georgia Hospital in Augusta, earning the Registered Nursing degree in 1956.

Following a brief tenure as evening staff nurse in the emergency department at University Hospital, I volunteered, in 1957, to join the Army Nurse Corps, entering the U.S. Army officer Training School; Ft. Sam Houston, TX. Women accepted into the Army Nurse Corps were not required to undergo the same basic training regimen as men who enlist. Instead, we became officers who took the leadership course that taught us the particulars of military life. For instance, I spent countless numbers of hours at the rifle range, mastering weaponry. I completed the medical evacuation training. I learned to perform tracheotomies (on goats and cadavers); learned to run a clinic and hospital ward, and to train corpsmen the range of skills that I was taught.

My career as an active-duty Army nurse engaged in full-time, year-round military service began officially upon my completing that training.

I received the BSN + Psychiatric Nurse designation from DePaul University; Chicago, in 1970.

My MA in HealthCare Administration came in 1972, from Governor's State University; University City, Illinois.

The academic segment of my training was crowned by an internship at the Forensic Center in Cincinnati and Saturday morning observations at the Cook County Jail, in Chicago. My Doctorate in Mental Health Administration from The Union Institute and University, Cincinnati, OH was conferred in 1979.

———

Following a nine-month, commuter engagement, I married 1st Lt. Will Curry, also a native of Athens, Georgia, **in 1958**. My new husband was the Leader of the U. S. Army Leadership School; Fort Gordon, Georgia. What a change in my life this was, being known as Ms. Lt. Ella A. Curry, the wife of a widower and father of two young children, Hallie and Willie Curry.

**First Lt. Willie M. Curry
and Lt. Ella Adams, Army Nurse Corps**

Initially Will and I lived on the Fort Gordon military base, Will in the officers' quarters while I occupied a space in the military nurses' quarters. A month after our marriage, we relocated to family-designated officers' housing on the base.

In 1959, Will received an honorable discharge from the Army and was assigned to the U. S. Army Reserve as Captain while I completed my tour of duty with the Army Nurse Corps.

When an opportunity came for Will to earn his Master's, we left Georgia and relocated to Tuskegee Institute,

Alabama, where as an undergraduate, Will had had the privilege of living on campus with the President of the college, Dr. Frederick Patterson and family.

Will pursued part-time studies for his graduate degree in Chemistry at Tuskegee and taught part-time. As an ROTC graduate with a Bachelor's in chemistry, a minor in mathematics, and a Master's in biochemistry, Will was appointed head of the Army Leadership School and served concurrently as a specialist in chemical, biological and radioactive warfare operations. I joined the VA Hospital Tuskegee, Alabama Hospital as a psychiatric nurse and general nurse educator.

We remained in Tuskegee for two years. Then Will found employment at Miles College in Fairfield, AL, as a science professor. I transferred to the VA Hospital in Birmingham, Alabama as a nurse on the psychiatric unit.

In 1960 we welcomed an addition to the family: Anthony (Tony) Curry. Then we were on the road again. My mission in joining the Army, after all, had been to avail myself of the means to complete my graduate education in Nursing/Hospital Administration—and to travel.

———————————

Our new place of residence was Chicago, Illinois. Will worked as a biochemist at the Northwestern University, Chicago Campus, and I accepted my first managerial assignment as nursing supervisor at the VA Research Hospital in the Chicago-Lake Michigan area.

A typical day in the Curry household started with

transporting our surrogate childcare attendants to and from our apartment on the South Side's Martin L. King Drive while Will and I adhered to our career paths.

Following Will's promotion to the University of Chicago Science Laboratories in 1963, we moved to the south suburbs of Chicago and enrolled in graduate courses at the University of Chicago.

With the birth of another son, Joseph (Joey) Curry, in 1963, we decided that our family was complete and that we needed a home of our own. We became residents of the multi-racial/multi-cultural city of Park Forest, Illinois, purportedly a model WW II conclave.

When Will's department chairman announced that he would be leaving his post at the University of Chicago, Will interviewed for a job as Section Head with Kankakee Illinois's Armour Pharmaceutical Company.

Needless to say, visions of my own unemployment danced through my head. After some soul searching, I decided to take a leap of faith: to leave the security of the VA Hospital and to apply for, and accept a grant from the State of Illinois and a stipend from the G. I. Bill. In return for these financial boons, I committed to work as medical personnel in the inner city or in rural areas of Illinois after graduation. This course would be a tremendous risk, but one worth taking. It meant that I would remain in public service for ten years, until about my thirty-eighth birthday.

My first job with the state of Illinois was as Program Director of the Inpatient Unit at the Tinsley Park Mental Health Center. Later, I was promoted to the post of Mental

Health Sub-Regional Director for the inner city area, serving a population of 800,000.

On perhaps the saddest day of our young marriage, the universe presented our family with a surprise that altered our reality. Less than a year in his new position with the pharmaceutical giant, Will was diagnosed with colon cancer. Fortunately, his supportive department chair, Dr. Sam Yanari, granted him a leave of absence. To Will's credit, he had recognized, early on, the value of investments, savings, mortgage insurance, and a comfortable nest egg— substantial financial assets—for the likely lean years. Even so, the care, concern, and help of Will's boss and colleagues Did more than yeoman's service toward returning him to good health. Their visits and lifts to work while he was on limited duty helped save our lives.

Thank God, my husband has been cancer-free for over five decades.

I kept my shoulder to the wheel, in the meantime, working as a mental health professional at a nursing home as part-time nursing supervisor, and teaching an evening class once a week at Olive Harvey College of Nursing. With nightly prayers and family support, I was able to manage my roles as wife, caregiver, parent, student, and career professional. In time, I learned that these crises and perils were not extraordinary, but merely the way of the world.

CONTENTS

EPISODE ONE

"A New Face, A New Force in Mental Health Care"

Manteno Executive Cabinet
Courtesy of Ebony Magazine; March, 1975
Standing: Dr. Ella A. Curry; First African
American Woman to head a
major mental hospital in the United States

"Mr. Speaker," The Honorable George M. O'Brien said to his fellows in the Illinois House of Representatives, "The state of Illinois is fortunate to improve its mental health services with the recent appointment of Dr. Ella Curry of Park Forest, Illinois, an experienced psychiatric nurse and administrator, to head the Manteno State Hospital, Manteno, IL. Thanks to the work of dedicated professionals like Dr. Curry, the importance of proper mental health care to our society is finally gaining the recognition it deserves."

Dr. Leroy P. Levitt, the Illinois Director of Mental Health and Developmental Disabilities, had passed the news on to me earlier: I had been selected as the Superintendent or Director of Manteno Hospital, approximately forty-eight miles roundtrip from my home in Park Forest, Illinois.

"I am very pleased to make this announcement," Dr. Levitt said. "Dr. Ella Curry is the first African American woman to be named as the top administrator at a major mental health facility in the United States. She brings to her new job great skill and commitment. Dr. Curry has done an outstanding job for the department of Mental Health. Whether working with community health groups or with state and local facilities, she has demonstrated both sensitivity to the needs of the mentally ill and her ability as an administrator. We are confident that as a registered psychiatric nurse with a doctoral degree, she will deliver the outcomes we so desperately need at this time."

The full speech appears in the February 27,1975, issue of *The Congressional Record*.

The Honorable George O'Brien, US Representative; District #6, State of IL, acknowledged my historic appointment on the floor of Congress, marking this phase of my journey a truly monumental event.

I took Representative O'Brien's and Dr. Levitt's accolades in stride. This assignment, I knew, would be a tall order, one certain to test my mettle, but I felt sure that I was up to the challenge.

I was so excited that the snow and chilly weather, ironically, brought a ray of sunshine to the Curry household. I called the exciting news out to my husband, Will.

"You've got to be joking," he said. "Congratulations!"

The next morning, I was greeted at my front door by reporters and cameras from the *Park Forest Star* (the local newspaper).

The first question from the press was, "Do you know that you are the first Black woman in the nation to hold this title?"

My answer was "Yes, and it is about time."

After speaking with the reporters for twenty minutes or so, I said, "I can't be late on my first day. Gentlemen, I will talk with you later."

As the snow continued to fall on a thirty-three-degree morning, I called out to my husband and children, "Let's get moving. We have a long drive down I-75 South to Manteno."

When I had a minute to catch my breath and think about it, the significance of this achievement hammered home. That I was being recognized for my unique approaches to mental health care was indeed a history-making event. Along with a long line of other trailblazing African American forerunners, I was creating history as the first African American woman to be named as head of a major state mental hospital in this nation.

With that groundbreaking announcement, the course of my life changed. My career as a health care professional was never the same. Promotion after advancement followed, with such speed that Will and I hardly had time to pause before one or both of us were being recruited for a new position.

————————

After forty-five years, I still remember my first day en route to my assignment as Director at Manteno.

The town was devoid of African American population except for the patients at the mental hospital and the staff that reported to duty there. What a change from my multi-cultural experience

It seemed to me that I was off to see the Wizard of Oz.

The reorganization of the Manteno Mental Health Center was the mammoth responsibility that could prove to be my undoing. Its restructuring entailed a reduction of the patient census of 1,300 to 500 over 3 years. No doubt, the challenge of depopulating a long-standing state mental hospital would be both vexing and daunting, yet the imperative to overhaul the system was long overdue.

Upon arrival, I received a professional greeting and the news of rumors that I might need an official escort--my race and gender possibly triggering concern regarding my reception in the community. I declined the offer.

I met, first, with staff, patients, and media, and visited the patient care buildings.

Next I had the first of what would become monthly cabinet meetings in the patient buildings, hosted by the program directors. I welcomed the administration, my team, and labor union officers as colleagues and professionals who could expect to have input or seats at the table. And

I stressed the imperative that all of us comply with equal employment laws.

Because winning staff cooperation and gaining the respect and admiration of my executive council would be paramount insofar as my management style was concerned, I approached the team with an attitude of leading rather than of commanding. In short, I set about encouraging the group to participate in setting goals and benchmarks and to collaborate with me as well as with one another.

After the first cabinet meeting I began to take a look at the adult patient programs. At the time, there were four: Admission, General Psychiatric, Geriatrics, and Alcoholism. The hospital officials wanted the reorganization of Manteno to put greater emphasis on an individualized plan for patient care. The former three-tier Adult Treatment Program would become one program with three different goals: short-term care (under 21-day stay); intermediate care (22-40-day stay); and continuing care (40+ -day stay). The exception would be The Community Placement Unit whose discharge goal was within 14 days. The managers in this last category were charged with working with the private sector in an effort to connect with family care, community group homes, and outpatient mental health clinics. The end result, we theorized, would be to reduce hospital confinement markedly.

Before I arrived, a patient's initial admission to Manteno for placement and treatment had been haphazard. Prospective patrons would be deposited together in one placc without regard for their disorder and without a clear-cut deadline for their discharge. Using clinical guidelines set forth by the psychiatric community, the admission unit, under my tenure, would be redeveloped with clinical evaluation as its purpose. Within ten days each new patient would land at an appropriate station, determined by his or her officially diagnosed or identified complaint.

Dividing the patients into diagnostic regulatory groups vs. into the former single-admission-and-discharge criteria would not only assure a sounder operational policy for the facility but also free up the staff to be trained to manage the new order professionally and expediently.

My pragmatic alternative plan organized the patients by criteria, i.e., short-term admissions with a length of stay of 10 or fewer days; an intermediate or adaptive behavior management patient group with a length of stay 30 or fewer days; a long-term patient group with a length of stay of 60 or fewer days; and a community placement group with a 45-day stay until these patients could be placed in community group homes, reside with family, or be accommodated in another viable aftercare plan. I assigned a cadre of staff known as mental health specialists to manage each patient group.

The Kankakee Journal and a variety of business and civic leaders printed articles reporting the changes at Manteno and invited me to their meetings to share what I believed were the improvements that we were making. When I accepted their requests, I was able to dispel rumors that admissions would cease and that Manteno would be closed. The weekend edition of the Manteno newspaper also featured a section called "The News and Views at

Manteno," in which the reporters had a field day helping to spread rumors surrounding activity at the establishment.

The adult psychiatric program, we decided, must safely screen its charges and commit to being operational by the end of calendar year 1975. This meant that consultants from other state mental health centers, such as the psychiatrists at private hospitals and those at the University of Chicago, were on loan to help us achieve that task in our restructuring mission. Because the geriatric/psycho-geriatric program seemed to be running efficiently, it was left intact and remained a part of the Nursing Home Industry, for the most part. Located in a recently renovated building, it was responsible for providing adaptive equipment and life-safety code upgrades. In addition, it retained its heavy emphasis on investigating placement opportunities for clients when feasible and boasted of having onsite rehabilitation services: physical therapy and occupational therapy for senior citizens.

The Department of Family and Social Services came to our rescue with this part of our strategy. Social Services provided home / health care assistance three times a week. In some remote areas, the family was required to complete a training class as home care workers. The family representative would be given a small stipend. The family could not use the funds to hire a friend or neighbor, nor could the family rep take on other employment. A case manager would make unannounced visits to the home and check on the patient and the care given by family members.

Since we had to certify a patient census of 865 beds, our thorough, comprehensive concentration on the Alcoholism

Program revealed a plethora of complications that would take a year to remedy in order to meet our goal. I observed, for instance, that we were experiencing an increase in the number of court-ordered admissions, overwhelming the court dockets and the Cook County Jail facilities. Until we could review this trend, I relegated our other focus areas to a quasi, sixty-day hiatus. When we investigated the cause of this explosion in the body count, we learned that the age range of this population was lower than Manteno had experienced in the previous three years. Formerly, a majority of this patient population consisted of males 35-68 years and a female patient group whose ages ranged from 18-55 years. Now, the group was swelling due to an infusion of younger clientele who faced serious lifestyle challenges, such as child abandonment, child custody, legal issues surrounding divorce, and a history of criminal activity.

Our examination of the circumstances surrounding conditions at Cook County revealed severe overcrowding at the jail, rumors of suspects' self-mutilation, outbreaks of fires within the cells, and several suicides. These calamities, as well as the increase in patient elopements (escapes into the village of Manteno without staff escorts) required my immediate attention. Such seemingly insurmountable problems all at one time were also frustrating my plans to increase patient-staff ratios. The village of Manteno hardly being enamored of this patient population, I had the responsibility of maintaining security as well as of securing treatment options.

I called an emergency meeting of the cabinet and made arrangements to visit the Cook County Jail personally with my chiefs, psychiatrist, nurses, budget and security personnel at my side. The crux of the matter became solving the problem of separating the mentally ill criminal offenders from the adults in the psychiatric treatment program. These were instances where a patient was found to be Not Guilty due to a diagnosis of mental illness. There were approximately 125 patients in this program, some of whom were found Not Guilty, but Mentally Ill, or Guilty but Mentally Ill. The latter group were often required to be accompanied from the hospital to court by security and treatment personnel. When a psychiatrist determined that the patient had responded to treatment, the individual would leave the hospital and return to the criminal justice system. The majority of patients who injured themselves and others were among this group and required trained staff to monitor them. When medical or surgical hospitalization was deemed necessary, we brokered agreements with local hospitals for care. And we compensated the local sheriff's department for the security that the officers provided the team.

Modifying the Alcoholism Program required a change in our expectations of the community. The majority of the patients were young people and women from Manteno and surrounding community. At first, the fate of the citizens who would have benefited from rehab was unfavorable due to the prolonged length of time and capital necessary for their convalescence and healing. Again, we had a stroke of good fortune. The hospitals in nearby counties were in nccd of revenue and began developing programs that would accept this population. When insurance or other methods of payment for this group were exhausted, hospitals referred them to the State, whereupon they were approved for detoxification procedures.

When Americans grew steadily alarmed at the rampant use of illicit drugs throughout the country, the Alcoholism Program became the Substance Abuse Program with the government allegedly waging a war on this problem that was threatening to careen out of control and devastate the nation.

Also under serious consideration on our agenda was a fifth or auxiliary initiative—a pilot to establish a forensic unit for court-ordered offenders. This unit would be under the jurisdiction of the criminal justice system. Law enforcement would provide personnel for security, the funds for transportation to and from court appearances, a psychiatrist, nurse practitioner/physician assistants, social workers, and legal staff to prepare the patients for training.

The staff located a vacant building near the security and safety office to host the pilot program and to prepare the patients for a potential move. In addition, measures for securing the building would be designed, then implemented

Once established, the program would give the court-bound offenders tips on how to prepare for their court appearance(s).

This new approach to the mental health field required staff retraining as well as family and community support. Such avenues assisted in providing alternatives to institutional care and treatment in the least restrictive of environments.

When my elaborate proposal for creating a tri-agency

program that I envisioned being co-sponsored by mental health, social services and women's advocacy groups was not approved, my team and I developed an alternate plan. We caucused to set up our Manteno pilot forensic program within sixty days, to serve only 125 patients. That smaller number would give us the opportunity to improve clinical patient-centered care and give us a path toward increasing staffing levels to a 1:78 ratio.

Dr. Myrene McAnnich, the Chicago Regional Mental Health Director, a colleague who knew me from my membership and presidency with the Lincoln Land State Chapter of the Association of Mental Health Administrators, became my mentor and a treasured friend. Her office location at the Water Tower Place was ideal for Saturday lunch and shopping on Michigan Avenue. We often exchanged particulars about sales, fashion, and styles. On occasion we shared accommodations while on professional travel. Possibly the most imposing professional contact with whom I've interacted in my career, it was Dr. McAnnich who encouraged me to continue with my studies for my doctorate. In fact, she gave me tips on surviving the oral examinations and recommended me for an administrative post at the Forensic Psychiatry Institute in Cincinnati, Ohio.

From Dr. McAnnich I learned of a renowned forensic program in Cincinnati, Ohio that seemed to be a promising model for our vision for Manteno. I traveled with her to study certain of that group's policies especially its approaches to handling security. I borrowed two ideas from the Cincinnati unit's program: (1) the use of double-lock doors to detain guests in a holding area until someone from the staff arrived to escort them into the Unit (rather than allowing outsiders to gain direct access to the facility); and (2) detaching the dining hall from patient areas and seating the patient-diners in three separate spaces. The most agitated patients required close scrutiny by staff because they sometimes started food fights and otherwise conducted themselves in a disorderly manner. They were issued disposable utensils. A second group required minimum observation and monitoring and had a space of its own. In a third zone patients who enjoyed near autonomy were seated.

The team members and I met to weigh our plans and timetables for setting our Model Forensic Unit in motion. I met, also, with the Union and the Equal Opportunity staff. To defuse skeptics' railroading or sabotaging our mission, I scheduled a patient-staff town hall meeting. To be certain that each citizen participated, my team recorded individuals' questions and assured them that if I didn't address their concern in my general comments, I would get back to them with answers. I wanted to schedule a retreat, but lacked the budget and the time flexibility to make that happen.

The forensic unit decided to develop a series of training modules that focused on alternatives to restraints and seclusion (i.e., show of force and behavior management techniques).

The practices then in use (leather cuffs and 2- or 4-point wrist and/or ankle restraints) were not the best approaches to prevent injury to the patient who precipitated the emergency and to others. Nor was locking a patient in a room with an observation window a wise course of action.

The specific guidelines for ordering seclusion and restraint dictated that the practice be used in the rare cases when patients and staff were in danger of being harmed, not as a form of punishment or as "time out" so that the staff could be temporarily relieved of their responsibilities, as a review of medical records for the Adult Psychiatry Program revealed. Ideally and ultimately mental health administrators should develop goals to treat crises in a restraint-free manner. I made it clear to all involved that Manteno was a hospital, not a prison; that the use of seclusion and restraint mechanisms be restricted. I deputized The Quality and Improvement Committee to monitor this activity monthly and to report any aberrant actions to my Clinical Deputy of Behavioral Interventions.

Exemptions to this rule, or fixed features, would remain in place, of course, for essential medical procedures when arm boards for IV's and casts for fractures to prevent falls were necessary.

The newly constituted forensic unit would be called upon either to enhance the Code Green Alert system or to create a new option.

(Under Code Green, security personnel, a nurse, and a team of six members of staff are summoned to confront a disruptive patient. Security's responsibility is to use a battery ram to pry open the door of someone who might have barricaded himself inside a room.

The team, which should be summoned early, before

the disturbance spiraled out of control, is responsible for securing the environment.

With them, the team carry a code green bag, containing adjustable cloth vest restraints; a gown, pajamas, a disposable sponge bath pack; and mechanical restraints.

The team designates a leader and selects a code word—a word that will be used to distract the patient from the bedlam that he is causing.

Three team members align themselves on one side of the patient and three on the other side. The team leader attempts to engage the patient verbally (talk to him or her, in an effort to deescalate the chaos.) If the behavior persists, the leader uses the code word as a form of indirection, to startle the patient and shift his focus.

When the six team members subdue the patient, the nurse administers medication approved by the chief of psychiatry (or an MD), or the team uses restrictive measures such as cuffs.

The group stays in place until the patient becomes compliant.) My training as a psychiatric nurse prepared me to develop a pocket guide for this technique.

———————

Through staff retirements and reassignments, transfers, and the eradication of sick leave abuse, we continued to admit and discharge patients and proceed to reduce the size of the work force. The nursing service helped by instituting a 12-hour, four-days-per-week schedule, all of which enriched our new initiative. When the labor union approved of the concessions we made in staffing, I opined that Manteno was well on its way to meeting the goals for outpatient treatment and community mental health development. At the same time that we addressed the issue of reducing staff, we continued to admit and discharge patients.

For all of our advancements and progress, the fly in the buttermilk arrived in April on Easter. I received an anonymous Easter basket in which there was a larger-than-life chocolate bunny. I accepted the gift and announced that I would raffle off the basket and give the proceeds to the patients' fund along with my sweet wishes.

In the spring of 1976, The Manteno Mental Health Center was in competition with several private providers and state mental health centers to be named Outstanding Mental Health program of the Year.

Illinois Governor Dan Walker hosted the annual mental health luncheon in Springfield. My boss, Dr. Leroy P. Levitt, Director of Mental Health, took the microphone and announced that a panel of former winners had selected The Manteno Mental Health Center's Alcoholism Program as the winner, for surpassing expectations. Governor Walker presented the award to me, and to Mr. George Flores, the Manteno Alcoholism Program Director.

Dr. Leroy Levitt, Illinois Director of Mental Health

Left to right: Gov. Dan Walker, Ella Curry, and George Flores

EPISODE TWO

The Paradigm Shift to Outpatient Care
at the Tinley Park Mental Health Center

When duty called next, it was in response to Dr. Robert Devito's request to name me to head the Mental Health Center in Tinley Park, IL. A paradigm shift from a 400-bed inpatient unit serving the South Chicago Metroplex to outpatient clinics throughout the Southside of Chicago would eliminate the cost to state government of maintaining outpatient services and reinvest the resources into community clinics.

Dr. Devito, who was the newly appointed Director of the Illinois State Department of Mental Health, convinced me that the position as Executive Director would be a logical and convenient fit for me and my family, located, as the hospital was, fewer than twelve miles from my home in Park Forest, Illinois. My commitment would be for approximately five years, until Tinley Park could be phased out. Of course, I liked the fact that this would be a promotion, but what was more appealing about the offer was the facility's proximity to home. It meant that I would enjoy dinner with my family for a change as opposed to being a glorified microwave-oven diva.

Ella Curry in informal setting

In his announcement of my appointment, Dr. DeVito explained that I would assume the duties of Superintendent. By way of background, he noted that I had served as the Sub-Regional Director for Mental Health on Chicago's Southside and had been recognized as the first Black woman in America to head a major mental hospital as Superintendent of the Manteno Mental Health Hospital. Dr. DeVito also mentioned my long-standing membership in the Association of Mental Health Administrators, where I had served for a number of years as president of the Lincoln Land Illinois chapter. Due to my familiarity with the community and its mental health providers, Dr. DeVito anticipated my bringing a wealth of administrative and programmatic knowledge to the position. "Hands down, Dr. Curry possesses the extensive background and preparation that qualify her to deal effectively with the complexities of this job," he said.

This assignment, interestingly enough, proved that a body can go home again. The majority of the Tinley Park staff had worked with me prior to my historic appointment as Head at Manteno. They had been my support system throughout my three-year tenure there. A few days after my arrival, I had a Meet and Greet with staff, patients, and community leaders. At a four-hour reception after I was formally on board, a large group of former associates and colleagues--including patients, community leaders, staff, and administrators--all showed up to welcome me back.

There was one problem with the new job at Tinley Park: my daughter-in law worked in the business office. As much as she enjoyed her job, her peers and superiors, I had to speak with her and her boss about the awkwardness of the situation. Under the circumstances, I could not afford to be accused of nepotism or bias. Her boss and I handled the delicate matter discreetly, finding her work with a different administrative district where she would actually be on an ascending career ladder. Wise young woman that she was, she had no objection to moving on. That decision, to remove a relative from the payroll, was my signal to the other employees that I was serious about fairness in the work place.

The Tinley Park assignment also taught me that elections have consequences. Now I had to contend with working with Illinois governor Big Jim Thompson, renowned for his work on the 9/11 Commission and for serving four consecutive terms as governor.

It was rumored that Governor Thompson was being prodded by his father, Dr. James Thompson, the new president of the Illinois Medical Society, to change the way that hospitals operated. The state was too heavily invested in inpatient care, the governor claimed. His father had negotiated with the Chicago area medical schools and universities to remove all of the limited licensed physicians from their posts, restricting their future practice in the state. This course of developments was a blow to these medical professionals whose careers had been shaped by their employment in public hospitals. Heretofore, the limited licensed doctors faced no impediments to their status as professionals; they freely diagnosed diseases, prescribed drugs, and signed medical records of all kinds. Now they would be demoted, reclassified as physicians' assistants and relocated outside of the Chicago area, for the most part, at a lower pay grade. If some were retained, they would be supervised by licensed physicians who cosigned their every action.

This blow was disturbing news to us in healthcare as well. We had expected to continue to rely on the limited licensed doctors to work with us as in the past, simplifying our duties and responsibilities.

From the governor's (and his father's) perspective, the change from the status quo was more advantageous politically, in that it helped Dr. Thompson gain favor with deans of medical schools, making it possible for newly graduated interns and retired medical staff to be employed in the city's most prestigious hospitals. We admitted that the Thompsons' proposal was technically appropriate, but we wrestled with the principle of the matter. After all, we had anticipated the Tinley Park Mental Health Center's becoming one of the three-county sites designated for the paradigm shift to a series of community mental health clinics.

Rumors spread throughout the area that Tinley Park Mental Health Center, along with other state mental health and developmental disabilities hospitals, was on the 'hit list" for termination. A torrent of outcries from leaders and representatives of organized labor and from the communities that would be impacted poured in. Their towns had also been identified as proposed clinic sites in the paradigm shift. Now those plans were being dismantled, and several state hospitals would have to be phased out.

The Department of Mental Health had already been in the process of developing a five-year plan to close the facilities when "Big Jim" took the helm, but their design was being disrupted by the governor's power play. Resigned to the course dictated by their fierce leader, the hospital's clinic directors went on a six-day retreat to work out the planned closures and reconfigurations before the governor's announcement.

Through back channels I heard that the special meeting at which the governor would reveal his plans and issue his ruling on health and mental health care was to be held within the week. The Community Relations staff began to make the rounds with local and state elected officials spreading the news that Big Jim Thompson would double-down on his decision to remove the limited licensed physicians from practicing, even under the supervision of licensed physicians and in some cases under the Chiefs of hospitals' medical staffs, especially in urban areas.

In mid-September 1978, the governor made his position clear: contingent with budgetary shortfalls, he alleged, his administration would phase down and phase out outpatient care and the paradigm would shift to community mental health centers.

For all intents and purposes, this change in power left me bogged down with politics and with misgivings and reservations about my charge. My time was being consumed with community protests and projections of how to manage the media. To address the latter concern, I hired a full-time media-savvy consultant to be my wingman at staff and community meetings. His duties were extensive: he reached out to residents who would be affected by the change that would follow the paradigm shift, scheduled town halls and invited the general public to show up. He published and distributed a monthly newsletter informing the residents of our plans and activities.

Nightmares about my inability to achieve the objective for which I had been appointed threatened to sideline me, especially after local young adult gangs--the Black Stone Rangers, The Temporary Woodlawn Organization, and The P-Stone Nation--challenged the flavor of Kool Aid I was serving. Their leaders told me, in no uncertain terms, that there would be "no government-crazy people" in their neighborhood. They backed up their threats by attending my town hall sessions and all but closing down the proceedings.

I knew that as long as we faced such sharp resistance from the community, the project to institute community outpatient services could not proceed. The patients' families and friends were to be part of the discharge planning process, but without access to affordable and convenient public transportation, they would be unable to participate in the requisite standard of care. Few if any of the citizens had automobiles. The Chicago Transit Authority did not serve the area.

The majority of the patients, after the initial assessment diagnosing the severity of their mental illness, were sent by bus from the Chicago Reed Mental Health Center, a receiving hospital near O'Hare Airport, to the Tinley Park Mental Health Center, and to Manteno Mental Health Center. Only patients and staff, including a nurse to administer medications and first aid, were permitted to ride this prison-fortified bus equipped with restraints, security windows and doors to prevent escapes. Twice a month, Black mega churches in Woodlawn, Hyde Park, and Calumet Heights provided passenger vans and drivers to transport relatives of their members in good standing to Tinley Park and/or to Manteno for service. Despite the transportation constraints that would limit patient support from family, I knew that I had to press on.

On the bright side was the news that interested entrepreneurs could apply for small grants from the state, and authorized banks would invest in the development of the shift to outpatient care on the Southside. Franchises like McDonald's and White Castle could enter into contracts with the government to locate in areas near the proposed community mental health outpatient services. The small businesses would then work with the Tinley Park vocational programs to train and hire our patients until they could find full-time employment.

No sooner had we taken some respite from our distress over the quandary we faced than we countenanced the disapproval of such arrangements by outpatient therapy professionals. There was a fear that Medicaid and the working poor would be eliminated from their caseload, affecting their steady revenue payees. "Nothing doing," they barked. "Not in our backyards will we tolerate mental health clinics, knowing the affliction that would follow," they droned.

One day I stopped by Tinley Park to pick up brochures and a film about the successful phasing down of institutional care in the national program model. I especially wanted to stress the implications that these tested, tried, and proven effective experiments would have for us at Tinley Park; I would focus on our expectation that funds from the original system would be reinvested in the community.

As the staff loaded materials into the state auto, my secretary came out of the building and told me that there was trouble at my Chicago office. The food and new furniture for the upcoming town hall could not be delivered because the gangs had taken over the office, were indeed staging a sit in, and the Chicago police were on site.

Before leaving Tinley Park, I stopped by the security office and asked security staff to accompany me to the Chicago office.

When I arrived, flanked by the police and security, the gang was ordered to retrieve my furniture from the middle of a heavily traveled parkway on Stoney Island and place it and other articles back in their rightful places.

The officers hauled the gang members off to the Cook County Department of Corrections. The lawyers who represented the mental health department and my staff delivered pictures of the damages to the station house. For their trouble, the "gangsters" were charged with reckless endangerment, theft of government property, and threats to employees at a government facility. I filed a report with the police and the lawyers handled the case.

When I rescheduled the town hall, the gang members, who were out on bail and accompanied by their attorneys, filled the auditorium. For an hour or more, I listened to them rant about their distrust of government. Several other community groups protested the intrusion of government in their lives also, especially following the Richard Daley era and the unrest during the 1968 Democratic National Convention in Chicago.

What a complex environment to discuss the needs of the mentally ill. The two unlikely bands believed that patients who had formerly been ostracized and rejected by elite facilities were now being courted and moved out of their own neighborhoods to be used as experimental subjects for the underutilized flagship psychiatric research hospital near the Chicago Campus of the University of Illinois.

I had an impossible time convincing the groups that their suspicions were ill-placed. The current options for citizens without insurance, I explained, were basically Tinley Park, a thirty-minute drive from the inner city and Manteno Mental Hospital, which was over fifty miles from the inner city. The new options for mental health care would be closer to patients' families and communities, I argued.

Still struggling to reassure the community, I offered to hold update-sessions in the neighborhoods and asked my audiences to tour Manteno and Tinley Park with my staff and me. I would spring for lunch and transportation, I promised.

I went to the extent of inviting former patients and family to take part in our community meetings. This offer was also rejected when hospitals out of the area began to repatriate patients from other semi-rural and remote areas of the state to take advantage of the amenities that we had offered the Tinley Park community.

Following the debacle between me, the gangs, and the police community, I accepted an invitation to be the guest speaker at the annual May Luncheon of the Police Chiefs and the Press. I was asked to address the unique interactions of residents, mental health entities, and police. In the May 4, 1978, issue of the *Star/Herald News* Outlet; Tinley Park, IL, Jay Feuerstein quoted me as saying that all of the professional training in the world cannot substitute for patience, compassion, and understanding when a citizen or a family with a mentally ill relative is seeking and crying out for help during a confrontation. I emphasized the fact that professionals best know how to neutralize potentially life-threatening traumas, but that the police also have an essential role to play in crisis intervention. The best police officers, I said, must undergo sensitivity training, possess flexibility, maturity, tolerance, and the ability to problem-solve in the presence of the mentally challenged. I ended my presentation with a few common sense tips and strategies for the pros and the officers.

Without the assistance and support of The University of Chicago and The University of Illinois, my team and I could not have accomplished our goal of closing the Tinley Park inpatient unit. The two institutions hired consultants to speak at our town halls. Once the town hall meetings gained prominence, neighborhood leaders, organizers, and attention-seeking politicians vied with one another to make appearances. This was a blessing to my media personality, to my chief of psychiatry, and to me! It meant that the media personality's role could be down-sized so that he could better manage other indispensable duties in his charge. It freed my chief of psychiatry from the duties of scheduling and overseeing town halls and open houses; now he would have the time to improve existing programs and establish new ones. It meant that I would no longer have to wear five hats. Finally, it meant that the heightened involvement and collaboration of interested and committed neighborhood residents could transform their environment.

After the Stoney Island, Jackson Park Hospital incident

with the southside gang bangers and the generous involvement of the two universities, community services for the mentally ill showed progress. Admissions to the Tinley Park Mental Health Center slowly but surely decreased, marking a major step toward Community Care for the mentally ill as opposed to Institutional Care, and the Tinley Park inpatient programs were quietly phased down and out.

EPISODE THREE

Start Spreading the News!
The Currys Are Moving to New York
The Bronx Psychiatric Center

Events on the home front rescued me from the memories of my satellite office at Stoney Island Parkway, Chicago, and the southside gang bangers debacle that had disrupted the plans for the Mental Health Outpatient Clinic.

In the winter of 1979, my husband Will presented the family with his relocation package. Armour Pharmaceutical had been acquired by Revlon Healthcare Group in Tuckahoe, New York, under "new rules." Will's department, Research and Development, was being transferred to New York, and my husband had received a promotion to the position of Section Head of their Biochemistry department. He would manage a group of scientists who isolated, purified, and developed therapeutic products from human blood for use in pre-clinical and clinical studies as treatment during the AIDS crisis.

I would follow, with two unhappy teenagers and

Princess, the family Alaskan Malamute in tow. Princess was a runaway queen who often terrorized our neighbors, which included UN diplomats and several celebrities like the late Ossie Davis and Ruby Dee. Before striking out for New York, we found Princess a happy home on a Connecticut Farm.

But that did not solve all of our dilemmas. I was dealing with a new home (in New Rochelle, NY), a new job, and an angry college kid left in Illinois, who one would think had been abandoned and was homeless. As far as my son was concerned, leaving sports and his friends was devastating, even though he had the adoring attention and protection of older, married siblings a few miles away. To him, this move meant that we were destroying this modern, All-American family. Will and I stood still long enough to show our sons that we were in charge and that with proper guidance, they would survive the family's move to New York.

Our son Tony remained in college in Illinois, and our younger son Joey began to adjust to student life at New Rochelle High School.

Life marched on as my husband settled into his new post as Research biochemist with the Revlon HealthCare Group that had acquired his previous employer, Armour Pharmaceutical, in a corporate takeover.

At first I saw myself as lucky, to land a position with the State of New York Office of Mental Health as Associate Director for the Bronx Psychiatric Hospital. This, I learned, was a far cry from the fantasy I had nursed of Sundays in the Park. The new appointment, in fact, required serious adjustments, as I was also attempting to learn Spanish and to ride the New York subway system.

The Mental Health Center at Bronx Psychiatric had recently removed a very popular African American psychiatrist and appointed in his place a Cuban-born psychiatrist who was affiliated with the Albert Einstein College of Medicine. The staff at Bronx Psychiatric was mourning the loss of their former Executive Director and required a lot of tender loving care. His defenders believed that his being sidelined was unfair. To be sure, the former executive director, who had also served as Acting Commissioner of Mental Health, had used poor judgment by appearing on television blaming Governor Hugh Carey for failing to provide resources to replace defective windows in the patient care area. The standard of providing locked/secure patient rooms could have prevented the patient suicides that occurred prior to the new executive administration's arrival. Instead of treading the bureaucratic waves that protocol demanded he navigate, the Director had let his impatience overrule his judgment.

My role in this topsy-turvy environment settled me in the lion's den between a Black male and the New York State Commissioner of Mental Health. I listened carefully to the various parties and asked staff to provide me with a copy of the incident report, the suicide-watch policy, and the policy-review minutes from the Quality Assurance Department.

In other words, I arrived at Bronx Psychiatric in the middle of a crisis—one that I had been hired to fix. What did this state of affairs tell me? Namely, that someone recruited for a job learn the entire story and terms of her employment—especially the existing conditions--before accepting the post. I had been so happy to relocate to be with my husband that I had gleefully and naively signed on while failing to consider the calamities that might face me at my anticipated "plum" appointment.

When I joined my boss, Dr. Pedro Ruiz, the new Executive Director of Bronx Psychiatric Center, and his staff, I began my duties as his Associate Director, primarily in charge of Community Operations.

The crisis at hand was the hospital's being slated for a visit from the Joint Commission for Hospital Accreditation (JCHACO). The committee responsible for recruiting me for employment had apparently noted the revelation in my *vitae* of my association and history with my former colleague, Dr. Myrene McAnnich, who headed the Commission's committee. Hence, the responsibility for preparing the Bronx Center for certification would fall to me, rather than to the new executive director, who was assuming his first directorship and lacked the preparation and experience to take on and manage the review.

I spent my first three months on the payroll getting my bearings. While priming the program for its certain evaluation, I faced several cases of chicanery and other types of reprehensible behavior. I observed, first hand, extensive staff absenteeism and shoddy record keeping in the form of incomplete and inaccurate medical files. In addition, I was made privy to rumors of rampant politicking, loan sharking, prostitution, and greed, which, purportedly, were the order of the day. As far as I could tell, the powers that be were consumed with lining their pockets at the expense of being the face, figuratively, of a valuable program whose aim should have been ministering to the needs of the country's most ignored patients and making the Center's job demonstrative of the care that that vulnerable population deserved. I wasn't on the job long before I realized that many on the administrative staff were not interested in the Bronx Psychiatric Center at all; indeed, several of the high-profile professionals hardly knew where the Bronx was!

My work was not just cut out for me; it threatened to be a feat of herculean proportions. Hence, I adopted the useful strategy that I had overheard my mother counsel someone take and implement at such pivotal times: "Don't ever let 'them' see you sweat."

As I struggled to finesse my family's relocation issues and with my own conversion to a New York state of mind, I met and became friendly with Dr. Carolyn Goodman, director of the Bronx Children's Center. I was immediately impressed with this colleague. Dr. Goodman was a great historian for the Bronx as well as a recognized clinician. I learned that her young adult son Andrew had traveled to Mississippi with James Chaney and Michael Schwerner, two fellow students, to register Blacks to vote. Unfortunately, Andrew and his peers were murdered by the Mississippi KKK.

Dr. Goodman and I discussed my plans for the Children's Center as well as strategies to get the Center accredited. She shared with me the staff's relief that I was uniquely equipped to confront this impending emergency triumphantly.

My first task was to appoint a team, which became

known as The Fort Bronx JCAHO Ambassadors. I ordered special identification tags and notebooks for the 10-person "squad". Dr. Goodman herself was a valuable agent, team player, and asset who swore to employ the necessary means to qualifying our 400-bed facility for state-of-the art status.

The next move was to locate a space that we could identify as headquarters.

Within 48 hours we obtained copies of the JCAHO Accreditation Standards. From Dr. Goodman I learned that each of the Bronx Psychiatric programs had been given a copy of the regulations for that department's area of responsibility alone. Before our initiative, for instance, the Nursing Department, which was a 24/7 operation, had received standards for the nursing area only. Now the Department had the other two areas' criteria as well. We organized a town hall-type meeting for the three work shifts (day, swing, and night) at which The JCAHO Ambassadors met and reviewed the citations left from the preceding JCAHO visit.

I returned to Chicago to meet with Dr. Myrene McAnnich, the Executive Director of the Joint Commission for Hospital Accreditation, to discuss and clarify the report from the Commission's past visit to the Bronx. We scheduled on-site pre-survey reviews of the patient care areas, state-operated outpatient clinics, and the support services.

My former colleagues in Illinois, I learned, often joked, "Where is Ella *now?*" The answer, at the time and for all of one year, was "Fort Apache, The Bronx," as the precinct was popularly called.

To our delight, we survived the JCAHO visit, with

the Joint Commission rendering The Bronx Psychiatric Center, accredited. The Center, which the Bronx District Attorney had denounced as a revolving door for murderers, was now on the right path to meeting its third-quarter timeline; change and help were on the way for The Bronx Hospital. The hospitals in the cities of Lincoln, Bronx, Lebanon, and St. Barnabas were the recipients of some of the new progressive measures. The outcome, hopefully, would be to decrease admissions for acute psychiatric patients by 120 individuals per month. The Bronx had long acknowledged several concerns, the least of which were window and heating problems. So the State Department of Mental Health proposed a $11.4 million to upgrade The Bronx Center and to enable improved staffing. Apparently, intermediate and long-term mental patients would be the core population.

When my Ambassadors and I were able to breathe a sigh of relief and lift our heads above water over the success of the JCAHO evaluation, Dr. Ruiz and the Bronx Psychiatric Center rewarded me with a three-day retreat to a conference of my choice.

EPISODE FOUR

On the Record: From Whistleblower
to Safety: The Willowbrook Story
Willowbrook Revisited: The Staten Island
Developmental Disabilities Center

Milestones and the Office of Mental Retardation, Relative
to Willowbrook, from 1967-1998.

Major issues and challenges from 1967-1987

1967 – 27000 patients lived on the Willowbrook campus
1968 – The Institute for Basic Research (IBR) was
    established on the Willowbrook campus to study
    ways to imporove the treatment of developmental
    disabilities. Investigators noted that prenatal tests
    revealed that Fragile X syndrome was thought to
    affect 16% of developmentally disabled males.
1972 – Robert Kennedy, then US Attorney General,
    visited the facility to observe the conditions. He was
    accompanied by TV journalist Geraldo Rivera, who

described the living conditions at the facility in a documentary.

The parents of 5000 children and young adults along with the New York State Association for Retarded Citizens filed suit in federal court to depopulate the Willowbrook facility because of substandard living conditions. The suit asked that the patients be placed in small community residences.

1974 – All state schools for the retarded were renamed Developmental Centers.

April/May, 1975 – Governor Hugh Carey signed the Willowbrook Consent Decree, which mandated that the state discontinue admitting patients to Willowbrook. The Decree extended to all patients under the umbrella of the NY State Office of Mental Retardation. The Willowbrook Consent Decree referred to the patients newly housed in community residences as "The Willowbrook Class."

1977 A separate Office for the Mentally Retarded and the Developmentally Disabled was officially established.

1978 –The first OMR/DD Commissioner was confirmed.

1978 – Hearings were convened to select and establish a community site for persons with disabilities.

1979 New Yorkers contributed to the development of day programs that allowed residents to have off-site outings for leisure, edification, and enrichment. Volunteers develop a program to serve older adult patients with 1600 in Day Programs.

1980 – As the newly appointed executive director of the

Willowbrook Project I appeared on ABC's *20/20* with Geraldo Rivera to discuss the status of compliance with the Consent Decree. In particular, progress with respect to community placement; living conditions; the hiring of more staff, medical care; prohibition of the use of restraints and requirement of appropriate clothing.

Geraldo Rivera, Former Willowbrook
Patient, and Dr. Ella Curry

My inspiration for this memoir was the opportunity to select and address the most challenging and dangerous obstacles that I faced as the first African American woman to head a major mental hospital.

For me, it was my tenure as the Executive Director of the Staten Island Developmental Center, formerly known as the Willowbrook State School; then The Willowbrook Class; New York (1980-1983).

At a press conference outside of Willowbrook in 1965, the late U.S. Senator Robert F. Kennedy described this facility for the mentally retarded and developmentally disabled as a "snake pit": "Many of our fellow citizens are suffering because of the lack of attention, imagination, and adequate manpower on Staten Island," Senator Kennedy remarked. "All of us are at fault; this facility is long overdue [for elevation to the dignity and pride that any institution housing human beings merits]."

According to Senator Kennedy, media exposes by *The New York Times, The Staten Island Advance,* and ABC TV's Geraldo Rivera heightened public awareness of Willowbrook's abysmal conditions in the 1970's and 1980's. These reports came on the heels of the class action lawsuit titled "New York State Association for Retarded Children, Inc, *et al.,* and Patricia Parisi *et al.* Appellees, v. Hugh L. Carey, individually and As Governor of the State of New York, *et al.,* Appellants, United States of America, *Amicus Curiae,* 596 F.2d 27 (2d Cir. 1979).

Their consciences having been pricked by the senator's stinging indictment, both the executive branch of government and the New York state legislature had the wherewithal to legislate for a sound program aimed at achieving the goals set forth in the aforementioned litigation and meeting the expectations of the State of New York Office of Developmental Disabilities.

Senator Kennedy's visit was followed by onsite inquiries by ACLU affiliates, representatives from the New York State Association of Retarded Children, and ABC news reporter Geraldo Rivera. The actions of these plaintiffs resulted in the parties entering into a Consent Decree with The State of New York Society in the 1970's. This decree assigned a Special Master to monitor the improvements and deinstitutionalization of the clients at Willowbrook to a less restricted environment closer to their families of origin.

In the early 1980's, I was appointed Executive Director of the Staten Island Developmental Center, formerly known as the Willowbrook State School, and accepted the responsibility to pilot this facility and its 1,300 clients out of the stormy wilderness of contention that had beset it for more than fifteen years.

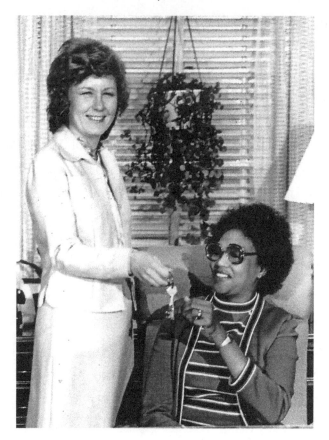

"Deputy Commissioner Elin Howe turns over the keys to the New York State Office of Mental Retardation and Developmental Disabilities to Dr. Ella Adams Curry."

The Developmental Disabilities Center was located on Staten Island, New York, approximately 42 miles, one way from my home in New Rochelle. Depending on the traffic on the George Washington Bridge, it could take me one and a half hours to reach the site. I used the commute as my time to listen to music or to tape my agenda for the day.

I had asked Ms. Elin Howe, the former Executive Director, to spend some time with me before she reported to her new post as Deputy Commissioner of Mental

Retardation in Albany, NY. She was excited and anxious to start as the first woman to hold the position. The two of us joked about being "twin firsts" in leadership roles.

During the first week of my new directorship, my husband joked, "This is your 'get out of jail' card," referring to my time as a consultant with the New York State Department of Corrections. My role there had been to assist the Deputy Commissioner with the development of mental health services for the prison system, using the skills I had honed at Manteno Hospital in Illinois.

The staff at Staten Island were excited and "ready to go to work." Following the Meet and Greet ceremonies with clients, staff, and professionals in the field, I placed a suggestion box in the cafeteria where I asked for ideas from staff. The most repeated recommendations, in addition to increasing staffing levels, were the development of pre-community placement programs, such as the activities for Daily Living Center, and the staff's desire to honor Elizabeth Connolly (New York State Assemblywoman for Staten island and Chairperson of the Narcotics Committee,1981-1990), with an office on campus. We addressed the last desire immediately by renovating a vacant building that had been the residence of former clients.

Knowing that the ACLU would be my shadow throughout this mission that bordered on the impossible, I invited representatives from that organization to the Connolly dedication ceremony (1982).

For the next two years, I tackled the work of meeting the expectations established by the Consent Decree: improving the conditions at the facility, establishing group homes and Pre-Community Placement Centers, and ultimately moving the clients out of this institutional leg of government to group homes and community placement units among their fellow citizens.

The process, which was created by the attorneys with the Central Office of Consent Decree Management, was a thoroughgoing, protracted one:

The first step was to inform the Centers and voluntary agencies that resources or funds were available and that they should submit proposals to be considered as recipients. In their proposals, they should state the allocations they needed and target priorities for their use. The staff from the Center would then meet with interested Providers.

Step two required Providers who wished to be considered for resources to submit a letter of intent, stating the history of their organization, other programs they operated, the agency's financial record, and how they would use the funds if they were approved.

Next, the Center staff would meet with the Providers to review their letters of intent.

Step four was a long one, in which the Center examined the applications carefully with an eye toward selecting the final Providers.

The Center then sent a letter of agreement to each Provider, asking the type of program they intended to develop, the projected number of beds they would offer and the level of care they would provide. Another detail would be a list of the names of the residents who were expected to be assigned to the Provider.

In Step five, the Provider developed and submitted a residential service plan.

The intense effort to locate a suitable property was the Provider's next task.

The Central Officer (OMR/DD) approved the cost estimates and the site itself.

In Step six, the Center reviewed the residential services that would be offered.

The property renovations would begin.

A Certificate of Occupancy from the city, town, or village needed to be granted.

A Sanitation Report from the city, town, or village would be provided.

A fire marshal from the city, town, or village would be approved.

****

My honeymoon as Director ended after two years, when my vision of Willowbrook/Staten Island and the forces that sought a contrary approach to meeting (or quelling) the terms of the Consent Decree collided.

As with previous directors, I received notice that Geraldo Rivera was planning to visit the campus to telecast its progress, on his *20/20* News program. He arrived earlier than anticipated, bringing camera crews and former clients of the Developmental Center. A strong scent of cleaning agents filled the air as Geraldo's crew began filming my staff at work dutifully transporting new mattresses from the Center's warehouse to the residential buildings.

When I arrived on the scene with the Center's A/V cameras, we began filming our visitors filming. I introduced myself as the new director and joked that the newsman had missed the ceremony that formalized my arrival in 1980. He ignored my greeting and quipped that he had caught me in the middle of housekeeping.

"Geraldo! I'm surprised at you," I said. "Did your mother not tell you to always clean up when you're expecting company?"

The journalist totally disregarded my crack on his "Got You" attack.

———————

A few months after Geraldo's visit and tour of the facility, I received an order to appear before Honorable Judge Robert Bartels' Court in Brooklyn, regarding compliance with the Willowbrook Consent Decree.

I was prepped for my court appearance by state attorneys from Governor Hugh Carey's office. The case was being heard at the Brooklyn East District Court.

The counsel for the plaintiffs began by establishing my credentials as an expert witness due to my twenty-six years of professional expertise and formal education as an Army Nurse Corps Veteran and a Ph.D. in Mental Health Administration.

My curriculum vitae was entered as an exhibit and approved by Judge Bartels. The attorney for the Center noted my appearance on ABC TV's 20/20 with Geraldo Rivera and recounted Geraldo's return visit.

The plaintiffs and the ACLU Attorneys asked if the Court-appointed Special Master's Report was accurately prepared in the Winter of 1982.

I had received that report from the Office of Mental Retardation and Developmental Disabilities, forty-five days following its completion. Commissioner Zymond Slezak and I were in the process of preparing a draft response that contained plans for corrective action.

The judge asked if I had a copy of the aforementioned draft report.

I answered in the affirmative; I had given a copy to my counsel the preceding week.

My attorney asked for permission to approach the Bench. He informed Judge Bartels that I had followed protocol on the Plan of Corrective Action; the plan would be released by the Commissioner's Office after review.

"How many patients have been placed in a Community Placement Residential setting in compliance with the 1987 Consent Judgment Stipulations in the last month?" Judge Bartels asked, "and what are the projections for the current month?"

I testified that the goal was to place thirty-five residents in 6-8 bed Community Living Arrangements with supportive work programs. At the time, only twenty residents had been placed within their borough of origin or interest. My office was in the process of training three families as Family Caretakers with Support Services. This program certified that the families had completed Family Care Training. Four Community Residences had not been approved by the local fire department or the local health department.

Now that Spring was near, I continued, the construction and renovations required to house the patient care residence and supported work programs would most likely have a better chance of meeting the goals.

At that juncture, outbursts from certain families and advocacy groups interrupted the proceedings. The Willowbrook authorities and leaders knew that the clients were being held at "Willowbrook" in deplorable conditions, they said, due to the Department's inability to make funds follow these "hard to place residents." The petitioners wailed that the clients were not safe, and in harm's way. In other words, citing the Special Master's findings regarding community placement, the attorneys for the plaintiffs were charging us with non-compliance with the stipulations of the Consent Decree.

The Judge had heard enough. He interrupted my testimony and abruptly discontinued the proceedings. To my surprise, he ordered the litigants and the ACLU to take a trip to Willowbrook/Staten Island as a group.

The Judge's startling reaction was in response, also, to accounts that he had heard of crying parents and siblings of the plaintiffs and complaints from the State Parent Association of Retarded, the advocacy arm for children.

Transportation was arranged, the courtroom was cleared, and I joined the entourage that traveled from Brooklyn to Staten Island. Enroute, I recalled the words of my late mother: "When under duress, don't ever let them see you sweat."

On that blistery, snowy day, we arrived via a thirteen, car-lane caravan.

The driver of the state car in which I was traveling signaled the motorcade that we would leave the caravan briefly, at which point we took a campus detour. We informed security that conducted entry to the facility that processing the group that accompanied us would take some time and that they should complete the process patiently and thoroughly. After being cleared, we waited at the residential buildings for the Judge and his Court to join us.

Much to my surprise, the facility was operating properly. It was clean, and the clients were in active treatment programs. (I learned later that one of the AFGE (American Federation of Government Employees) union reps from the Center had been in court with us. Upon hearing the judge's order to the officers of the court, plaintiffs, and defendants to head for Staten Island, the union steward had telephoned the facility and the staffing office, and Housekeeping had swept the place cleaner than the Board of Health could have made it.) In other words, all was well at the site, contrary to what the Court was alleging.

Judge Bartels was met at the building entrance by the building manager, the physician, the nurse practitioner, the charge nurse, and the onsite program staff. Most of the clients were having their afternoon snack, and several were engaged in projects. After the judge spoke with the staff and some of the patients, he appeared to be satisfied and was about to leave without observing the claims of current and future neglect that had been charged against the Center. Before departing, he insisted on visiting the vocational building where higher functioning clients were housed.

Fortunately, there was not a single "gotcha" moment. On the Judge's authority, the members of the court were instructed to be present in court at 10 a.m. the following day.

The next morning, I was back on the witness stand explaining the process of acquiring community placement sites, which according to my philosophy was the best approach to the standard of care when other options were not available. The judge acknowledged my testimony then stated that I was temporarily dismissed, but subject to recall. The attorneys for the New York Department of Developmental Disabilities were called to the stand next.

I spent the weekend at home with attorneys preparing me for recall.

The next week, the director of the governor's Office of Public Affairs sent the late Tim Russert, NBC News anchor, to my office to give me and the staff further guidance on dealing with the media. I told the gentleman that my mother's advice "not to let them see you sweat" and my own instincts were as sound guidance as any that he imparted.

During subsequent months, I determined to investigate the suspicions that had resulted in Willowbrook's being a constant target of inspection. I began to make rounds during the evening and night shifts, even to the point of taking up residence in an apartment on the campus.

As I drove to the onsite garage after the lunch hour one day, I noticed that I was being followed by an unmarked black automobile with an unidentified person wearing a black leather jacket inside. Why had gate security allowed a strange vehicle to bypass the closed and guarded entrance, I wondered. After I had a brief encounter with the driver who had trailed behind me, an employee who had witnessed the exchange advised me that all was well. Even so, I exited my automobile, parked, and went to the garage to check out what had happened.

Moments after arriving at my desk, I overheard a request from the front gate to speak with me. Visibly shaken, the employee, whose name was Antonio, said, "Lady, Ms. Dr. Curry, do not follow unidentified vehicles or people again. It's dangerous You could have got us killed."

When Antonio left, I reported the event to my boss at the NYC Regional Office and summoned the Deputy Director and Security Chief to my office. I notified them of the front gate incident and took the rest of the day off.

––––––––––

Some time later, rumors circulated that the driver and his passenger were "known persons involved with organized criminal activity." I notified my superiors and instructed investigative personnel to provide me with a report after they spoke with the employees familiar with the incident.

For my safety and security, an escort was assigned to me on my routine campus rounds. In addition, I was directed to move from the apartment that I had been occupying to a hotel near the hospital after routine business hours.

Rumors were not in short supply about other disturbing events suspected at the facility, some current, some past.

There was an account of an employee's domestic violence history, for example. A married couple's argument had resulted in a homicide/suicide. A nurse was purportedly found in a shallow grave near the campus.

Along with suspicions of drug dealings, alcohol abuse, and prostitution, I knew that hospitals, like other 24/7 operations, could be breeding grounds for all kinds of unlawful activities.

In fact, tips of drug deals involving staff while they were actively assigned to client care and services reached me. Over time, the authorities estimated that the "drug operations," which were the work of individuals alleged to have organized crime connections, netted over $500,000 per year.

One afternoon I received an anonymous tip that some of our employees regularly locked our clients inside a state car outside a bar while the employees caroused inside.

I asked the caller's name and address and whether he had telephoned the police.

The local police and hospital safety officers were sent to the location. Security checked out the report through the Center's Missing Patients policy.

Indeed, two patients were missing, but they had been seen leaving with staff. The security log indicated that they had gone to a store, but had failed to sign in at the security station when they returned.

The patients were examined by the medical staff and found to be unharmed. Staff who had taken them offsite were interviewed by HR and reprimanded by the supervisory staff and personnel management. I asked whether it had been past practice for staff to sign patients out for trips to the mall or to shopping centers. This was not policy, according to personnel management.

Another cause for concern were the series of locked tunnels on the grounds that were formally used during inclement weather. I heard that employees were using them for sinister purposes.

Far too many bizarre and unexplained incidents were happening to go unchecked, I decided. As a result, I increased my personal involvement in unraveling the mysteries, adding Saturdays and Sundays to my surreptitious tours.

Several higher-functioning patients assigned to the vocational shops began to signal me to be careful, that "bad things were going on." Often my source for such information was "Janie Doe," who frequently spoke with the administration and me about messages from the grapevine. "Janie" was aware of what she referred to as "something goin' on," "bad deeds"—booze, drugs, and money for sex. Before I consented to hear her reports, I made sure that it was safe for her to speak with me in my office. I promised to keep her secrets, but told her that she was to spend more time in the Willowbrook clothing boutique, her assignment in the community placement program.

The backstory about Janie was that, though a gentle and harmless snoop, she had a history of flirting with male staff. Before I documented the evidence of my investigation, Janie was discharged from Willowbrook.

Heeding the words of caution from multiple sources, I decided to spend some nights in my apartment, some in the hotel near the campus, and still others in the comfort of my home in New Rochelle, approximately forty-eight miles from my office on Staten Island.

Under the pretense that I was preparing an audit, I reviewed the personnel records of the suspects, made copies of their file photos, and secured my "research" data off the hospital campus, in my safe deposit box. Through the chain of command, I passed my findings on to the NY state government and requested that undercover agents investigate the incidents that we could document.

I learned that a minor cadre from the undercover operations would be assigned to the campus as contract painters, interior designers, and telephone repair installers for the audio/visual needs of the clinical and support services. Later, when a fire was set near my personal quarters as I prepared dinner late one afternoon, I requested that undercover agents surveil the area and my home in New Rochelle as well.

With that action, I began to get death threats.

The mischief was growing more and more aggressive and consuming so much of my time, that I requested a meeting with the commissioner and the head of the NY State Police. They reported an overall change in the conditions at Staten Island. As the patient census was being reduced, they noted, staff incidents of lawlessness were increasing. Undercover agents were then hired as contract building and trade staff as well as grounds crew.

In the spring of 1983, I began to receive telephone threats of harm to my family. Following leads into the matter, the authorities arrested several of the 1,800 employees.

During the criminal trial of the allegations against the

former employees, my husband and I were advised to spend some time in Europe.

Local media speculations on the state of affairs at Willowbrook led to accusations of a lapse in management and with "blame the bureaucracy" banter. Even then, I was not to be deterred. I reported my suspicions of a growing drug distribution problem among a small group of the Center's employees to New York City Regional Director, Mr. Thomas Shirtz. They were confirmed by NY State troopers and noted in the Friday, May 29,1983, of *The Staten Island Advance*.

When the truth was finally known and told, I was revealed as a whistleblower, running, for my safety, from criminal elements.

After being called "the clean-up woman" and other derogatory names, I was advised to consider entering the witness protection program. I opted to do on vacation until things calmed down. This stressful experience forced me to revisit the lessons that I learned from The Dignity of Risk concept:

1. Recognize that a problem exists.
2. Get a clear picture of the problem.
3. Search for solutions to the problem.
4. Decide on the best solutions that can be achieved with existing resources.
5. Plan to implement the solutions.
6. Carry out the plan.
7. Evaluate the results.

8. Practice decision-making
9. Know when to ask for help
10. Learn from experience.

Despite our efforts to do all in our power to meet the expectations set forth in the Consent Decree, in 1972 the federal court of Brooklyn made the decision to close Willowbrook.

by Ella A Curry, Ph.D.

In looking back over my experience as director at Willowbrook, a tremendous sense of the unique professional challenge still remains with me. The greatest satisfaction of the health care professional, particularly for those of us who serve the mentally disabled, is to insure quality, humane treatment in the least restrictive environment possible. The triumph with the clients of Willowbrook is that, once the truth was known, and the commitment made by the State of New York, the best was indeed delivered to them. Negative notoriety no longer will be ascribed to Willowbrook, because now it positively represents the best direction toward community based services for the mentally disabled.

It was my personal privilege to serve as director there.

Ella A. Curry, Ph.D.

"A Promise Fulfilled". The closing of "Willowbrook"

The closing of Willowbrook gnaws at me still. As I look back over my experience as Director there, a sense of the unique professional challenge I faced remains with me. The greatest satisfaction of the health care profession, particularly for those of us who serve the mentally disabled, is to ensure quality, humane treatment in the least restrictive environment.

Our triumph with the clients at Willowbrook meant that notoriety would no longer be ascribed to that campus.

The State of New York talked the talk and walked with rapid speed to enshrine the facility with the best knowledge toward community-based services known at the time. It was my personal privilege to serve as its one-time Executive Director.

———————

The time I spent with the New York State Department of Corrections Service as a mental health program consultant prompted the Commissioner of the State Department, along with other state officials from Governor Hugh Carey's office to recruit me for the position of Executive Director of the Staten Island Development Center. Friends who had worked with me in the Chicago area also approached me about taking the Commissioner's offer seriously.

Several outreach telephone calls and lunches inquiring about my interest in the position on Staten Island followed. In addition, the former executive director of the Development Center, Ms. Elin Howe, who was being promoted to Associate Commissioner for Developmental Disabilities, joined ranks with the others o persuade me to consider the job. Ms. Howe lauded the perks and compensation for the distance I would have to travel. She did her best, also, to prick my conscience with her idea that the patients at the Center and their families "needed my help." Ironically, as a caregiver, what I secretly craved was just to be wanted, needed, and appreciated.

When Ms. Howe discussed my replacing her, I made it clear that I would not take the job, if offered, without knowing more about what it entailed. I insisted that I would have to read the job description and to know if it was strictly adhered to.

A colleague of mine would be leaving with Ms. Howe as her aide in her new position. He said that the offer to replace her would not be made unless and until I visited the facility and met with the staff, union representatives, and parents of the facility's residents. Eventually I toured the campus and consulted with fellow members of the National Association of Mental Health Administrators.

The search committee arranged a lunch meeting with me at which I felt no pressure to accept the position. A month later, I met with the members of the committee again and accepted the job with caveats: provisions for transportation, an apartment on the campus, and a list of creature comforts.

Thus, after a year at the Bronx Psychiatric Center, I arrived at Staten Island as Executive Director of its Developmental Center, vowing to get in the trenches to serve the mental health community, all heart, gusto, and obligation.

EPISODE FIVE

The Westchester County State
Developmental Disabilities Services Office

When I returned from Europe, I asked to be reassigned. To my delight, I was placed at The Westchester County State Developmental Disabilities Services Office, located in Tarrytown, NY, as the Executive Director with an inpatient unit on the grounds of the Harlem Valley Hospital in Wingdale, NY. This office was fifteen minutes from my home in New Rochelle in comparison to the hours-long commute to Staten Island.

The county of Westchester was unique for the times, in that it enjoyed a state/county partnership. New York did not have an inpatient residential development of community group homes and vocational supportive programs for the developmentally disabled. The mental retardation and Harlem Valley Mental Health Center, located in Wingdale near the state of Connecticut, was the site for clients who had their roots in Westchester, awaiting placement in the community group homes that were under development.

Several of this client population were former Staten Island Developmental Center alumni.

****

At Westchester, I received the following
awards and citations.
Award for Outstanding Community Service;
United Way of Westchester County
White Plains, New York;1986

Citations

Citation for Outstanding Achievement in
Community Placement of the Clients from
Community to Group Homes and Services; 1986

Westchester County Development
Disabilities Services Office
White Plains, NY; 20 January 1986
Nomination: Director of the Year by the New York
State Office of Mental Retardation and Developmental
Disabilities by Commissioner Arthur B. Webb,1986

EPISODE SIX

The White House Summit with
US Secretary of the Department of
Health and Human Services

In 1985, Armour Pharmaceutical Company, where my husband Will had worked as a research biochemist for twenty years, was acquired in a merger with "Big Pharma," located in the Washington, D.C. metro area. Will was transferred with his company, and I moved with him to the nation's capital, of course.

That Fall, Department of Human Services Secretary, Margaret Heckler, invited twenty-five top women executives in the health field to attend a week-long summit at the White House to collaborate on the direction of health care in the nation. As President-elect of the Association of Mental Health Administrators, I was among the experts who came to the attention of HHS. In addition, the summit would have at its disposal a pool of potential candidates who might be recruited to take positions in the Reagan Administration's cabinet and sub-cabinet.

ASSOCIATION OF MENTAL HEALTH ADMINISTRATORS

NEWSLETTER

The Professional Association for Administrators of Services for the Emotionally Disturbed, Mentally Ill, Mentally Retarded, Developmentally Disabled and those with problems of Alcohol and Substance Abuse.   OCTOBER 1985

AMHA president-elect Ella Curry meets with former HHS Secretary Margaret Heckler.

White House Summit 1985

On the second day, the group was assigned "handlers" for the recruitment effort. My handler, to my surprise, was The Honorable Betty Heitman, Co-chairperson for the Republican National Committee. Since the Reagan administration had no Blacks or other minorities in his cabinet, I wondered what the group had in mind for me, the lone African American participant in the Summit.

The Honorable Mary Jo Jacobi, Special Assistant to President Ronald Reagan, introduced Secretary Heckler, whom, rumor alleged, the President was considering replacing. The secretary welcomed the group and discussed the interface relationships between the White House, Congress, and the President's cabinet members. Following her presentation, our agenda for the week was announced, and we were treated to a reception with select members of the President's cabinet, Congress, and their staffs escorting us to a dinner buffet, hosted by Co-chair Heitman.

After breakfast the next day, we were assigned to groups and specific tables. The first order of business was to inform us of The Target 80's Program, a highlight of the Summit and Margaret Heckler's brain child. The Program's mission was to form a talent bank of women with a strong interest in and commitment to HHS's mission.

I was seated at the table with Republican Senator Orrin Hatch, a known crusader for conservative values, a foe of the Equal Rights Amendment, and an opponent of a woman's right to choose. My history of political activism might not allow me to survive an assignment with this group for a week and sit at the same luncheon table with a fellow citizen who had such "plantation views" of women and minorities. Nevertheless, I bit my lip and soldiered on.

At lunch, I felt a shoe repeatedly stroking my leg. I left the table for a few minutes to freshen up and to get my bearings. When I returned, I found the proper moment to confront the aggressive character who had made contact with me. "The next time you touch my leg," I said quietly through clenched teeth, "I will snatch you out of that seat and slap you so roundly, your ears will ring." The "gentleman" neither acknowledged my rebuke nor resumed his unwelcome harassment.

The remainder of the afternoon, the group had the pleasure of participating in a discussion with Congressman Bill Gadson of Ohio, the ranking member of the Ways and Means Committee. The congressman praised the group highly, emphasizing the fact that we women of distinction had a key role to play in establishing the new reality—that healthcare was no longer a social service, but a "business." The marketplace now dictated that bids for Medicaid/Medicare Services were necessary in order to close the gaps in long-term care.

All of the participants expressed their apprehension about the proposed three-year plan to deal with the escalating cost of healthcare. I voiced my concern that since only 11% of GNP was spent on healthcare, providers would move away from demanding quality care and settle for cost-based services. At the time, we were in the midst of addressing long-neglected women's health issues and the immediate AIDS crisis.

The good news was our recognition of vaccination compensation as a vital step toward the prevention of illness. It appeared certain, also, that drug export laws would require enhanced standards compliance rather than contracting for low-quality medicine from nations whose products too many American pharmacists dispensed. The U. S. had no input in the research that developed standards and oversight mechanisms for the production of drugs. We agreed that we needed to support efforts to expand a cost-effective Home Healthcare Bill and to review the malpractice legislation that would address the high cost of primary health care.

Congressman Gadson was seeking our help in drafting amendments to existing Medicare and Medicaid policy. Both programs needed to be restructured to close the long-term care gaps. At the time, the private sector was demanding relief from the requirement that non-third party payors for long-term care be relegated to the public sector. The majority of this long- term-care patient group did not have the assets or the insurance necessary to cover such health care costs. We were asked our opinion regarding this issue.

The Congressman recognized my hand. I explained that when the private sector controlled long-term care, beds were reserved for the patients who required rehabilitation services. This kept private agencies in compliance with the existing federal non-discriminatory regulations clause. For example, an 80/20 mix, with 20 beds reserved for rehabilitation would be less costly than protracted hospital stays. That arrangement would provide for short-stay rehabilitation with continued care in Home Care Agencies. I recommended using Senior Care Grants for pilot programs that might tell us the validity of this possibility.

Congressman Gadson appeared to like the idea. During the break, he approached me about sharing my views with his staff. I informed him that my background being Mental Health and Nursing Administration, the 20/80 patient mix would limit the number of beds to one wing. Rehabilitation therapists and rehabilitation technicians who would man the wing would be more cost-effective than employing a nursing staff, which would dictate a 24/7 staffing pattern. As a start, the patients who comprised the 20/80 setup could also return for outpatient therapy, using a day hospital model. The lessons I learned from my experience in Illinois with different models of care with a focus on program primacy were proving highly useful and serving me well, I surmised secretly in self-congratulations.

The group suggested that we work toward executing a change in the public and political perception of "welfare" programs. Currently, we decided, healthcare is too often seen as a discretionary-dollars matter, not as an entitlement.

The HHS Secretary appeared distressed to learn that the patient safety guidelines required by the Health Care Financing Administration would not be enough to keep the citizens' trust in providers. Unless safety procedures were stated realistically, specifically, uniformly, and in a timely manner, the citizens would begin to question the actions of healthcare policy makers.

On the third day, Co-chair Betty Heitman, my handler, asked me to join her for a private lunch. I accepted her invitation. Right away, I discovered that she and I had two separate agendas. Hers was to recruit me for a sub-cabinet position in Mental Retardation and Developmental Disabilities. If interested in the appointment, I would have to resign my political affiliation with the Democratic Party and sign on as a Republican.

My life course demanded my loyalty to and pride in the party of my lifelong affiliation—the Democrats. At that stage in my career, I had no interest in becoming a pawn of "power, politics, and greed."

For the remainder of the Summit I listened to the presentations on supporting the proposed Three-Year HHS Plan as it related to my professional concentration. I was especially interested in the latest information regarding the AIDS crisis because my husband was working with his group at Revlon Pharmaceutical, examining the isolation, purification, and development of therapeutic products from human blood.

Afterwards, I was grateful for the opportunity to have participated in the Summit. I was anxious to share what I had learned with Will and my colleagues, at the 1985 Annual Meeting in San Francisco, where, as the new President of the Association of Mental Health Administrators, I had a suite overlooking the Golden Gate Bridge and my personal butler, both of which accentuated my overall pleasure with the White House Summit.

EPISODE SEVEN

The Kingsboro Psychiatric Center
Brooklyn, New York

A house search, aided by Washington, D.C. clinical psychologist Dr. Gladys Baxley, settled me and Will in temporary quarters in Falls Church, VA, approximately seven miles from the White House. I became a consultant to the Capital Care Health Group in their quest to expand service to the prison population; namely, ways to introduce the monitoring surveillance system for house arrest. Dr. Baxley was helpful, also, in helping me start my own consulting firm, Curry & Curry Associated, Inc. With her generous assistance, I met a plethora of DC professionals in the mental health field who sought to revise our approach to mental health services.

My tenure with the Capital Health Group lasted only seven months. As a result of a great deal of lobbying by colleagues, friends, politicians, and the Executive Director of The Kingsboro Psychiatric Center, I was offered a deal that I should have turned down in light of my history as "the fixer" for all manner of mismanaged and crumbling programs. Despite some misgivings, and convinced that I could be of service--needed, wanted, and appreciated--I returned to New York as "Boss Lady" (the moniker, I learned, that had secretly been assigned to me by former staff and associates). In spite of the reservations I claimed to have about the characterization, I had no real qualms about living up to that reputation.

This move to New York meant that I would live in an apartment on the Kingsboro Center grounds until I found permanent housing.

My Kingsboro assignment proved to be the first and only serious test to my then thirty-three years of wedded bliss. My husband and children were not too keen on my spending weekdays and nights in New York and weekends in our East Falls Church townhouse. I saw the change of premises as an opportunity to advance my retirement goal. I had left New York before, just two years short of being eligible for full retirement benefits. Now I would earn those additional credits and qualify for a complete and satisfactory pension package. For a while, Will and I didn't complain about our commute and housing arrangements; we told ourselves that this was temporary; that we would work the plan that would deliver us to our vision of being empty nesters soon.

The downside was that every Friday night, either I would fly from New York to Washington National or Dulles Airport; or Will would either drive to New York, or take the train from DC to New York Central Station, to Brooklyn; then take a metro bus and taxi cab to the Kingsboro Psychiatric Center.

During a snow storm on one of Will's shuttles, the cab driver asked his destination. When Will said The Brooklyn Psychiatric Center, the driver told him that he would not be going onto the hospital grounds. He left Will at the gate to the facility. Security contacted me and I approved Will's transport to my apartment. The signs of Will's resentment and displeasure with his plight were all too evident when he delivered an ultimatum: that I find a residence close to the George Washington Bridge entering the city. I obliged him by moving into a townhouse formerly owned by Rita Hayworth, with a view of the Statue of Liberty. I justified the extra expense for housing with the quip that the money was being wisely spent for a deserved outcome: a well-funded retirement package in two years.

This arrangement continued until Will's early retirement and his accumulation, after four years, of an abundance of frequent flyer miles that our children were all too happy to use.

Among the first items on my agenda at Kingsboro were meetings with the staff and Board of Visitors, a group of mental health advocates from the community, and with the group's president who was the uncle of Senator Chuck Schumer (the dean of New York's congressional Democratic delegation and Senate majority leader, as of November 2020). With these interested parties I shared a story board, spelling out how I planned to close a perilously unsafe building whose violations risked the safety of patients and staff. The building had no working elevators which were imperative for delivering the patients' equipment, supplies, meals, laundry, and medicine. In fact, floors 8-10 were boarded up. Mr. Schumer knew of my involvement in exposing and remedying the deplorable conditions at the Bronx Psychiatric Center, reported in a *Weekly NY Times* article.

I needed the Kingsboro group's help in meeting my responsibility for the lives of the 220 patients and staff whose wellbeing depended on the full functionality of Building 10. With my new outreach liaisons, I mapped out a plan for transferring the patients housed in the ten-story building and closing it. Mr. Schumer agreed to grease the political landscape and schedule a series of meetings with the Brooklyn Contingency, a coalition of local politicians and merchants.

Next, I met with the labor union chain of command and pleaded with them to give me three months to review the stack of grievances that they had issued prior to my arrival, the foremost of which was their fear that the layoff of 1.78 staff and the subsequent cancellation of support services would be a nightmare for the Borough of Brooklyn. The battle for Brooklyn was on. I asked the union leaders to trust but verify, of course, my years at Willowbrook. I assured them that the staff would be accountable for all of their actions. Guilty parties would be punished for non-compliance if allegations against them were confirmed. It did not help that several of the former staff from Willowbrook, still seething from the aftermath of the punishment incurred by their cronies who were indicted and sent to prison, were now working at Kingsboro. In the face of that bitter opposition, I made it known in no uncertain terms to the union officials and the governor's office that I would not accept the weight of retaining staff without the ability to transfer the patients and close the patient care building.

The process I envisioned for the patients' transfer included moving them as a group to under-populated mental health centers. To prepare for this major shift in location, my staff and I scheduled a series of one-on-one meetings, Mondays through Saturdays, from 9 a.m. to 12 p.m., between me, certain Kingsboro cabinet members, and the patients, their families, staff, healthcare providers, politicians, and labor unions. When some of the parents and significant others did not immediately meet with us, our social workers and case managers offered alternative times to accommodate them, 12 hours, four days a week, staying from 9 until 10 p.m. M-Saturday.

From the Kingsboro staff, I requested ideas on where we stood in view of the labor relations challenges. An absolute reductionin staff was the mandate of the Director for Operations and Budget. His question was how we could mount a campaign to maintain the staff and arrive at a patient staff ratio of 1.78 as opposed to the .98 staff plus 10% for administrative and support services. The word on the campus was that the poorest section of Brooklyn would suffer layoffs and that the community merchants would be forced to close. Because this would not be a desirable outcome, I requested help from the Regional and State Office of Mental Health and struck a deal in which I succeeded in getting 98% of what I requested.

To design and implement the tasks before us, I scheduled a retreat and hired a consulting firm to help with public relations. Union representatives, the NY State Commissioner of Mental Health, negotiators from the State Office of Mental Health, contributors from the governor's office, and officers of the Citizens Board of Visitors all joined together at Montauk, Long Island to help save Kingsboro.

At these assemblies we fashioned an atmosphere for the logistical resolution of screening, linking, and planning for each of the designated patients to lodge in safer accommodations. The social workers' chief and his staff were dispatched to meet with their counterparts who had been designated to receive the patients. The Upstate NY Psychiatric Centers also became active in the planning. Their staffs met with Kingsboro patients, and the NY State Office of Mental Health office picked up the tab for families to visit residential in-patients monthly for one year. Many family members had never flown on a commercial airline, or visited Kingsboro, even though several resided only a few subway stops from the neighborhood.

We held a series of town hall-like meetings with patients, staff, vendors, and organized labor to collaborate on the matter. These preliminary sessions consumed more than two months. With the expert help of the Kingsboro staff and their fellows at the destination locations screening and linking the patients, our expectation was that the residents would be settled in their designated facilities before the start of the Christmas holidays.

My office arranged for staff wishing to remain at Kingsboro be allowed to do so. Those who preferred reassignment to another patient care service could be transferred. Much to my surprise, when staff members saw the locations where the patients would take up residence, several of them requested transfers, to be with the patients.

That feat met with cheers from the labor unions.

I myself relocated to a vacant apartment on campus. My husband Will visited me every weekend except holidays. Of course, the two of us kept in touch daily by telephone.

Prior to the meetings, retreat, and town halls, I told myself that I would resign if this mission failed. I would return home and enjoy my eight o'clock coffee from the A& P with my Krispy Creme donut, and continue to gain weight. I wrote my letter of resignation before convening the planning sessions. In it I stated that I could not in good conscience be responsible for the 700 patients and staff without the immediate actions of transferring the 220 patients to existing vacant beds and programs that would be a safer environment for care and treatment.

In the end, Building 10 was demolished, and with the political attention garnered for that mission, I learned how to gain the cooperation of a number of disparate entities.

Our final achievement was a patient voter registration drive before the primary election of 1988. Bus transportation was contracted, and patients donned their "Sunday Best" attire and were on their best behavior at the polls. The Kingsboro social workers and case managers deserve special recognition for the success of that initiative. When the New York legislature heard about our push to register all patients who met the eligibility requirements to vote, this group of citizens had a cause to celebrate a new-found source of empowerment.

For my efforts at Kingsboro, the governor's Office of Employee Relations presented me with The Labor-Management Achievement Award for 1987. The one achievement that went wanting, I confess, was an individual patient care plan. Otherwise, my appointment to Kingsboro was another "mission accomplished."

Citations and Awards

The Governors of New York State Labor-Management Achievement for the Closure of Building #10 and the smooth relocation of patients to Upstate Centers

(by Governor Mario Cuomo, 1987)

Citation for Excellence in Mental Health Service; Kingsboro Psychiatric Center

(by the New York State Legislature,1988)

Recognition from the State Association of Community Mental Health Centers

The William (Bill) Byron award for excellence in Mental Health - June1989

The Community Mental Health Caring Community, naming the Group Home

The Dr. Ella Curry Group Home

EPISODE EIGHT

A "New York State of Mind": The New York City Regional Office

Now that the transfer of 220 former Kingsboro Psychiatric Hospital patients was a mission accomplished, the building that formerly housed the patients was finally demolished, due to the cost of restoration and the decline of the patient population.

I was off to my new post following the recommendation of my former superior, Deputy Commissioner of Mental Health, the late Dr. Alice Lin, an Internationally acclaimed Health and Human Service guru. I was promoted to the New York City Regional Mental Health Director, formerly housed in the Two World Trade Center. This— the responsibility for the adult and Children's Psychiatric Center for the five boroughs (Manhattan, Bronx, Queens, Brooklyn and Staten island)--was the pinnacle of my successes.

At the time, the Mental Health Office was located in the former #2 World Trade Center on the 52nd Floor with a view of the Statue of Liberty. There was no doubt in my mind that this was a most fitting career climax--as close to heaven as I would ever be.

Before I could relax and enjoy the view from my swanky quarters near the East River and the Statue of Liberty, the homeless, mentally ill, and dual-diagnosed patients suffering from drug addiction plagued Grand Central Station and the Port Authority. For the good of the State of New York, all state leaders, on one accord, joined in the battle to save Manhattan from the plague of drug addiction. To tackle this war, my office established a "tripwire operation" to deal with the overcrowding in the New York psychiatric hospitals. This operation was coordinated by a cooperative agreement with the following partnering agents who deployed teams to the casualty sites: Emergency Medical Service, The NY Police Department, the State Drug Abuse Programs and The Intensive Case Management System. *The New York Times* and TV News Media kept the city and state on alert.

Thank goodness for my spouse. The weekend flights/ train rides to my home in East Falls Church, VA became a one-way commute for him. The only perks were free or reduced Broadway tickets or dinner at Two World Center on the 110th Floor on rare occasions. "Princess" that I am, nobody had to tell me that this was Paradise.

During the second year of my sojourn, my father was diagnosed with terminal prostate cancer. Flashbacks of not being at my mother's deathbed when I was a teenager haunted me; I vowed not to let this happen again. I left my post to be at my father's side and for once in my life, put family first. Six months later, I returned to New York as Senior Deputy Director for the Office of Substance Abuse. Shortly after I resumed my post, my father passed away, with my sister Lacy Johnson and her mother, Queen, Daddy's wife of a few years, at his bedside.

My father, Benjamin Franklin Adams was a professional tailor and later in life a Union Steward for the Amalgamated Poultry Industry for forty years. During his retirement, he embraced his passion—fishing--a 5-time weekly obsession. I returned home for the interment.

Mr. Benjamin Franklin Adams (d. 1989)

After I returned from my father's funeral, I faced the challenge of moving patients from the New York City psychiatric hospitals to four state psychiatric inpatient centers, in Manhattan, Queens, the Bronx, and Brooklyn.

After several meetings with Dr. Sarah Kellerman, the New York City Commissioner and Mental Health Director, I informed my superior, Dr. Alice Lin, that I had finished my work at the Kingsboro Psychiatric Center.

———————

To begin my duties at the New York Regional Office would require an increase in budget for personnel and equipment--$1.6 million dollars to start.

The major New York City hospital was Bellevue, which was located in Manhattan. The facility would not sustain itself without additional funding, especially since Bellevue and the other mental health providers needed the budgetary increase in order to focus on reducing the inpatient population and re-investing the originally allocated funds to expand our Community Outpatient programs.

Dr. Lin discussed the situation with her boss, Dr. Richard Surles, the State Commissioner. Dr. Surles had Dr. Lin and me contact Ms. Anita Haynes, a social worker whose premiere Discharge Coordinator program we would adopt. Ms. Haynes agreed to serve as our consultant for the Intensive Case Manager program then proceeded to train the staff for all of the state psychiatric centers except Staten Island (we lacked the necessary data to justify funding to include Staten Island in this pilot program).

I informed Dr. Lin that I had received a high volume of telephone calls about overcrowding in the emergency room at Bellevue Hospital. The callers complained that the staff had been unable to transfer psychiatric patients from the inpatient unit.

One evening, I asked my driver to stop at Bellevue in order to see the problems first hand. I felt like a Geraldo Rivera clone from my Willowbrook days as I entered the hospital. Wearing my white medical coat with my name and title on the top pocket and a copy of the license for the service to operate, I found patients on hospital stretchers in handcuffs and in some cases, foot restraints. I asked my escort about the patients who required assistance, such as those in the Activities of Daily Living area, patients who needed food, fluids, and help using the lavatory. I asked to see either documentation of the patients' discharge from the ER to the inpatient unit or for procedures for the discharge-planning process.

Then I asked my escort to have the evening supervisor meet me at the inpatient unit. I asked her for the Policy and Procedures Manual. After scanning the section on admission and discharge from the unit, I found that the census was higher than the stated unit capacity. Moreover, a majority of the patients were undomiciled (had not been placed in a nursing home).

When I arrived home, I telephoned my boss to report my findings.

The next morning I brought my deputy, Mr, Doe," up to date. "Mr. Doe," who was responsible for the licensing unit staff, was a political appointee who had experience

with both the City of New York and the City Health and
Hospital systems.

The next evening, Mr. Doe's wife called and confided
that her spouse had been hospitalized due to a history of
alcoholism. I assured Mrs. Doe that I would manage as
her husband convalesced and that she should be concerned
only with his health.

I informed the staff that our deputy was in the
hospital and that we needed someone to assume his duties
temporarily. Of the two individuals who submitted letters
to be considered, I selected the staff member who was best
qualified to advance with the project.

Next I asked for volunteers willing to train and
get the Intensive Case Management Program up and
running. Four teams were assembled and assigned to the
Manhattan, Bronx, Brooklyn, and Queens boroughs.
Each team consisted of eight staff members: three social
work supervisors; two RN's; two vocation rehabilitation
counselors, one principal psychologist, and an on-call
psychiatrist from the state mental health hospitals. All team
members had a pager, a state credit card with a budget as
allocated by the Deputy Regional Director/designee.

I did not go home to East Falls Church, VA the weekend
after I chose the interim deputy. Instead, I sat in the bay
window of my new "digs" and read the *New York Times* and
watched the ships sail down the East River.

While Dr. Lin was feeling the heat from letters from my
agency and from the NYC Hospital directors, my focus was
on training and getting the Intensive Case Management

staff out and about the City. I relieved some of Dr. Lin's anxiety to start with Bellevue Hospital after she received training from the consultant.

Although the staff was somewhat excited about this new initiative, I made no major changes until my deputy returned. The remainder of the week I spent discussing what if any exposure our endeavors would bring to our legal department. I prepared a Memo of Understanding for the legal department's review. They suggested that we incorporate my need into a confirmation agreement. To the best of my recollection, the agreement with Bellevue Department of psychiatry went as follows: Dr.Kellerman: If the Health and Hospital Corporation determined that further efforts to locate a community placement for a patient would be futile, the patient should be discharged and transferred to a state psychiatric center.

If I recall correctly, the Intensive Care Management program became popular with the vendors. The mentally ill were not to be visible near the United Nations Headquarters in Manhattan. Even the drug dealers knew when the United Nations was in session and helped clear the area of the homeless and drug users.

The typical behavior of a derelict is exemplified in the following experience:

One evening my deputy and I were walking near Grand Central Station. It was starting to snow. I saw a large box moving down the street. My deputy knocked on the cardboard box.

"Who's there?" came a voice from inside the box.

"It's beginning to snow and you should relocate to a dry area," we answered.

"What's wrong with you people?" the voice inside the box said. "Do you think I'm crazy? I will go and find myself another box."

We moved away from the box and went inside the terminal to summon NYPD.

An officer accompanied us back outside and proceeded to call the name of the person inside the box.

"Leave me alone," we were told for our trouble.

According to the case manager on site, the man was harmless.

———————

With the help of the homeless and street people who were substance abusers, activity in and around the Port Authority, the airport, and other tourist points of interest began to decrease, but not disappear. I congratulated the ICM staff on a job well done. The last time I checked, in 2015, the program was still in existence.

EPISODE NINE

The Lone Star State: Houston City Limits

In the fall of 1991, I registered as a patient at the Michael DeBakey Veterans Hospital in Houston, Texas. It was time to undergo a thorough physical examination to assess my readiness for the second phase of my life's journey. I felt comfortable being examined and treated at the VA since I had completed my military service with the agency as a vet in the Army Nurse Corps. In fact, I credit the VA with giving me my first job of note—that of Veterans Administrative Nurse Executive. The diagnosis was: orthopedic issues in my knees and lower back.

While undergoing testing at Debakey, I met the professionals, associates, and contacts who would become my new friends. Members of the local chapter of the Women's Veterans Organization visited me. Apparently the group was in in its infancy, capable only of distributing creature comfort items to newly admitted male veteran patients. "Gloria," the local chapter president, a former WAC, traveled on her motor scooter to spend time with me daily. Recalling having seen my photo in an issue of *Ebony Magazine*, Gloria outed me as a nurse. My new ally and advocate, who was well known to the staff and patients, made sure that I received the VIP treatment, often referring to me as "Dr. Ella from the North."

Prior to my discharge, I was recruited to become a lifetime member of Chapter 9 of the Women Veterans Organization. I began attending the group's monthly meetings and volunteered to work with the homeless women veterans group. I was tasked with outreach work, giving the women tips for job interviews and collecting attire for their job searches. I must say that I enjoyed visiting the women vets and children, in some cases, at Houston shelters and hotels where they were housed for up to three months. These services were sponsored by the city of Houston with the VA supplying visiting nurses each week.

Being somewhat familiar with my *vitae*, the chief of the nursing staff asked if I might consider joining them. I told her, quite candidly, that a consulting role after settlement in the area would interest me. (I was not sure that my husband and I would choose Houston as our final and permanent home, even though the reason for our relocation was that two of our children and our grandkids had lived in Houston for several years.)

After my discharge from Debakey, I met with Ms. Lottie Lockett, the nursing supervisor of psychiatric services and gave her my application for a management position.

A few weeks later, I was contacted about accepting a position as the Assistant Chief of Nursing for Psychiatry and Ambulatory Care.

After I had served as Assistant Chief for fifteen months, my supervisor, Dr. J. Devance Hamilton, was promoted to the VA Houston Chief of staff. Dr. Hamilton asked me to become the first-ever-non-MD Associate Chief of Staff, responsible for operations and expansion of the satellite clinic programs in the Houston and catchment areas. My duties were to develop outpatient services aimed at decreasing veterans' travels to Houston and reducing the expanding patient census.

During the 1999 Joint Commission on the Accreditation of Healthcare Organization's visit (JCAHO), the Galveston and Conroe clinics were operating up to standards. But the VA clinic in Beaumont had received several building violations and had been cited for problems with the limited licensed physicians' lack of supervision. As for the VA satellite clinic in Lufkin, it required improvement of its mental health services due to staffing problems and its policy of using contract psychiatrists only.

When I accepted responsibility, the Clinic supervisor in Beaumont was a licensed social worker who had relocated from the Houston VA to Beaumont. I discovered that staff morale was low and that stronger leadership was needed. Veterans throughout the region were bypassing the clinic and traveling to Houston for routine primary care. To address the problem, the VA Regional Office decided to expand and place the clinic closer to Interstate Highway I-10 East. The former clinic leader resigned, although the gossip was that he did not "jump ship," but was pushed.

The clinic had strong political support as well as support from the VFW and the American Legion. Within fifteen months, U.S. General Services located a site near an existing medical complex. Planning for the facility and its construction took over nine months. The opportunity to work with the veterans' group and vendors was exhausting, often requiring me to spend two to three days per week onsite and eventually requiring the staff to travel to Houston once a week as well.

Some flagship clinic operations were veteran-friendly, permitting veterans to benefit from teleconferences with Houston medical specialists, for instance. My staff and I were able to arrange for supplies to be delivered by van to the clinic, and for transportation for Houston veterans scheduled for major surgery or overnight hospital stays. The social workers had access to families of cancer patients receiving day treatment on weekend visits at The Fisher House on the grounds at the VA Houston Medical Center.

For my husband's part, he found exciting ways to enjoy retirement. In addition to spending time with his children and grandchildren, he benefited from my overnight stays in Beaumont, playing golf at the Municipal Golf Course and staying ready at a moment's notice to visit the Golden Nugget in Lake Charles, LA.

Prior to my retirement, I recruited a well-qualified primary care physician as the Beaumont VA Clinic Director. I myself resumed making bi-monthly visits.

I remained in the position of VA Associate Chief of Staff until my second retirement in 2000.

My experience with the Houston VA
netted me several awards:

- Cerificate of Commendation for my Leadership of the VA Access to Clinical Service Team, 1998.

- Award from the Department of Veterans Affairs Office of the Inspector General (OIG); Washington, D.C.
- Special Contribution. In recognition of my service to the special Task Force Assigned investigating the conditions noted at the VA Hospital; Northport, New York, 1999.
- VA Houston- Veterans Homeless Program for Outstanding Service and Dedication.
- Veterans Affairs Appreciation for my tenure as Associate Chief of Staff for operations and expansion of the satellite clinic programs in the Houston area, June 2000.
- The VA Medical Center presented me with the Black Heritage Award for Outstanding Accomplishments during Black History Month; 2000.

———

Since entering the world of Retirement in June 2000, I have restricted my professional endeavors to limited Healthcare Consulting, at LLC: Curry and Curry Associates, Inc., for the most part.

Together, Will and I established this consulting firm, Curry & Curry Associates, Inc. I founded the firm formally in 2001 and serve as President and CEO. The principals in the firm have more than half a century of expertise in the HealthCare, Quality Management, Pharmaceutical and Clinical arenas. Our client base includes the Cention Pharmaceutical Co.; Kankakee IL; The Lone Star College System of Houston, Kingwood, Montgomery, and Conroe,

Texas, The Michael Debakey Veterans Affairs Medical Center; Houston; Baylor College of Medicine International Affairs; and The Second Home for Senior Adults.

The firm lists as former clients a four-year contract, with the Cention Pharmaceutical Company of Kankakee, IL; a six-year contract with the Lone Star College System Nursing Program of North Harris, Montgomery,Kingwood, and Conroe Texas. The Michael Debakey Veterans Affairs Medical Center Houston and The Second Home for Seniors Adult Day Care Services in Spring, Texas. a contract with the MD Anderson College of Medicine; and with the Baylor College of Medicine International Partners, for Team Building; and a contract for the recruitment of select clinical/administrative personnel interested in employment with the VA Medical Center in Houston, Texas.

For the past twenty years, I have had the pleasure of getting to know my family better, going to family reunions, hosting friends and neighbors, going on cruises and otherwise traveling with my grandchildren, playing Bridge, and cooking. Recently I took time away from my activities to write my memoir.

I am truly blessed.

EPISODE TEN

Family Ties

The Lucien and Hallie Dorseys. Our only daughter, Hallie; PhD (Biblical Counseling); MA (Economics). Retired regional auditor for the State of Illinois Department of Internal Revenue. Her husband, **Lucien**, a retired computer programmer for the Utilities and Banking Industry of Houston, Texas.

Christopher Dorsey, the couple's son, is a former Marine, and a criminal justice professional. Christopher's wife **Sarah Dorsey**, is an assistant principal with the Aldine School District in Houston. Their three adorable children are **Davian, Brayden**, and daughter **Aubriana.**

The Andre and **Eutora Valmores.** Andre is Hallie's adopted god son. Andre works on Wall Street and **Eutora** is an elementary school teacher. They have one son, **Lenox.**

The Doctors Ugo and Faith Ihekeweazu. Faith Dorsey Ihekeweazu is Hallie and Lucien's daughter. Faith is a research pediatrician at Texas Children's Hospital located in the world renowned Texas Medical Center. **Ugo** is an orthopedic surgeon with the Houston Fondren Group. Their daughters **Noel** (5) and **Grace** (2) are enjoying their Zoom classes and story time with their grandparents.

<u>The Willie and Lynce Currys</u>. Our eldest son **Willie** retired from the FDIC as a supervisor of banks and savings and loan companies throughout the U.S.

I give a Special Tribute to my daughter-in-law, **Lynce**, my #1 Hero. In *Lynce's Perfect Peace, Reflections of my Journey with Multiple Myeloma*, Lynce chronicles her journey from **diagnosis in 2017 to** her present-day treatment with photographs, events, a strong religious support system, great medical care, and prayers. The proverb that guides her daily walk --"I don't know what tomorrow holds, but I know who holds tomorrow"--is taken from the gospel song, "I Know Who Holds Tomorrow." Prior to retirement, Lynce worked for IBM, then left to start her private company: Leading, Learning, and Living until 2017.

Willie and Lynce's daughter **Kimberly** is a skills specialist in the Aldine-Westville School District in Houston. She is still single. Hint...hint.

Willie and Lynce's son **Kevin** and his wife **Beverly** are newlyweds, enjoying their first home in Katy, Texas. Kevin is a procurement manager for Virco, a corporation that supplies operational equipment for schools, churches, and other venues. Beverly is a registered nurse practitioner for pediatrics at the Texas Children's Hospital Clinics.

The Anthony (Tony) and Carolyn Currys. Tony, our second son, is a computer engineer who has been employed with the BMC Software Company, Houston, for over twenty years. A true multi-tasker, Tony is a scout master and a safety officer for the Black Skier's Club; a former hockey player with the Long Island, NY Club; motorcyclist, and "jack of all trades."

Tony's wife **Carolyn** is a critical care recovery room nurse with special skills assisting heart-lung transplant patients. In addition to her nursing degree Carolyn holds a B.S. in Biology. Carolyn has been employed at the St. Luke's Hospital in Houston for forty years.

Tony and Carolyn are the proud parents of triplets. To rear triplets takes a town, city, state, and nation. I can confirm that, as a retired senior citizen grandma. In 2019, the family was featured in the 'Energy Corridor," a Community Living magazine.

Neo is an eagle scout, a *cum laude* graduate of the Strake Jesuit Academy. Currently he is enrolled at The University of Houston, in pre-law. He is a debate coach and nation-wide judge for high school and college teams. He was featured in the 2019 annual National Eagle Scout Yearbook and in the 2020 Houston Energy Corridor Magazine. His project reported the development of "The Library in the Park" project in West Houston. This library is used by children and parents for story time.

Kaley is a Westbury Academy graduate and is currently attending the Savannah College of Arts and Sciences (SCAD) located in Savannah,GA. She has sold paintings as a sketch artist, and will have great input in developing the cover design for my memoir, with my publisher.

Trinity is a graduate of the St. Agnes Academy in Houston. Trinity has won several local and state tennis championships. At Baylor University in Waco, Texas, she enrolled in ROTC and studied Kinesiology. She has resumed her studies at The University of Houston.

The Currys at home at the Lakes of Parkway Estates, located in West Houston, near the Energy Corridor.

I have saved the most traumatic event of my life for last. Our last-born son, **Joseph E. (Joey) Curry,** was called to heaven in 2014. His sudden death has been the "perpetual bewilderment" of my existence.

Joseph "Joey" Everett Curry

I still have flashbacks of the Sunday morning when I received a call from my son Joey's friend Dawn. Through crushing sobs, she was saying that the EMT's were at Joey's condominium. Out son was not breathing.

When Will and I arrived, we were greeted by the Harris County sheriff, who said that the medical examiner was en route to make the formal pronouncement that our youngest child was deceased.

I was speechless and in a state of shock. My husband began to call our other children to tell them the news. As I prayed, I tried to keep from fainting and from screaming.

"Don't ever let people see you sweat," I could hear my deceased mother say. Gaining strength, I traded my tears for family hugs while greeting the medical examiner with an air of professionalism and a "stiff upper lip."

Will and the other men in the family remained at the scene, and the female family members escorted me home. I was in emotional distress; I had lost my youngest child.

Known as "Joey," and affectionately called "Uncle Joey," Joseph Curry was born in Chicago. The certificate from Joey's autopsy, dated 4/6/2014, reads as cause of death: Dilated Cardiac Hypertrophy due to Hypertensive Cardiac Disease. My child was merely fifty years old.

Everyone who knew Joey remembers his giving nature. A big brother to all of his nieces and nephews, he taught most of them and every other youngster who was interested, to play chess.

Joey's hobbies and interests qualified him as a young renaissance man. He was an accomplished cross-country runner, a music connoisseur, a voracious reader, an avid sports fan, and a collector of memorabilia.

A communications graduate of the Montgomery College in Blue Bell, PA, Joey worked in the music, audio visual and computer industry. His nieces and nephews continue to enjoy his valued Prince Collection along with his store of music of other famous artists. His clever spirit continues to be a blessing to our fond, cherished memories.

———————————

As most of my family and friends have made the transition from visits and Sunday brunch with their parents, grandparents and great grandparents, we have adjusted to celebrating birthdays and holidays in Zoom sessions and drive-by greetings. My personal motto is, we all need someone to love, something to do, and something to look forward to.

Please enjoy the attached video, featuring family fun at my 80th Birthday Celebration. The video was done by my son Tony, family and Friends. I am respectfully looking forward to your reading my Memoir.

80th Birthday celebration Link:
https://drive.google.com/file/d/1try8fzFDD4Hdg444.JjrhDcpMEbCyiME4l/view